If you sometimes—
- scream at the kids before breakfast is half over
- feel that your mate doesn't understand you
- would like a new self-image
- can't love your mother-in-law, or someone else
- seem unable to communicate with your children
- feel that living has no purpose

Then you have a kink or two.

THE KINK AND I is a book for you.

It will help you identify and correct the kinks that keep you from being the human being God intended you to be.

Then you'll discover the joy of untwisted living!

JAMES D. MALLORY, JR., M.D., a practicing psychiatrist, has since 1970 directed the Atlanta (Ga.) Counseling Center, offering professional therapy within a distinctively Christian frame of reference. He is a graduate of Princeton University and received his medical degree from Duke University's School of Medicine. After internship at Duke, Dr. Mallory became a flight surgeon and chief of the Air Force Clinic at Orlando Air Force Base, Florida. He later returned to Duke, completed a residency program in psychiatry, and served for a time as Assistant Professor of Psychiatry. Dr. Mallory is married to the former Betsy Tippett, and they have four children.

STANLEY C. BALDWIN is a writer, pastor, and counselor. He is author of *Games Satan Plays,* an editor of Power/line papers (Scripture Press), and editor of Victor Books.

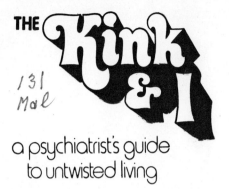

THE **Kink & I**

131
Mal

a psychiatrist's guide
to untwisted living

JAMES D. MALLORY, JR., M.D.
WITH STANLEY C. BALDWIN

While this book is designed for the reader's personal enjoyment and profit, it is also intended for group study. A leader's guide is available from your local bookstore or from the publisher at 95¢.

Published by
VICTOR BOOKS

a division of SP Publications, Inc.

Third printing, 1974

750027

Library of Congress Card No. 73-78688
ISBN 0-88207-237-4
© 1973 SP Publications, Inc. World rights reserved.
Printed in the United States of America.

Contents

TO ALL OF MY PATIENTS, who have taught me so much: I want to assure you of confidentiality in the many case histories that are presented here. All the names are changed; the situations are altered; identifying characteristics of people are switched around so that no one can be identified or embarrassed.

Some of you will think you see yourself in a particular story, but I remind you that there are many people going through the same trials, tribulations, and experiences.

James D. Mallory, Jr.

Part I

What Are We Doing To Each Other?

1

Sticks, Stones, and Words

Betsy was a ding-a-ling. At least, that was the image my wife tended to project as a teen-ager.

Take the episode of the referee's flag, for example. Betsy was a cheerleader for her high school. All she knew about football was that at periodic intervals you yell. Once, near the sideline where Betsy stood, a referee dropped his flag to signal a penalty for some infraction in the game. She thought he had dropped his handkerchief. Betsy picked it up, thinking she would return it when things quieted down a little bit. The referee was not very appreciative of this gesture.

The whole episode gave the crowd, particularly Betsy's friends, a good laugh, but it also tended to shape and encourage the ding-a-ling or screwball image. Even though she was intelligent and sensitive, Betsy developed this style because others reacted pleasantly and gave her affirmation of a sort.

Sometimes we encourage and affirm the wrong behavior and attitudes in people. This is done very commonly with children. We may laugh good naturedly at a cute little rascal's tall stories, four-letter words, or stubborn "No!" when he's told to do something.

But we must ask ourselves in all our relationships, "What are we doing to each other?"

Hurtful Affirmation

The question is not, "What's the easiest response at the moment?" It is not, "What is my natural reaction?" The question is, "What will be the long-range effect of my reaction to this person?" Will it have a positive or negative impact? Will it be helpful or hurtful, constructive or destructive?

George helped virtually to destroy his beloved wife because he did not understand this principle. He constantly gave his wife positive feedback for being a pretty, helpless little girl. This is what he always reinforced. If she were about to put a piece of bread into the toaster, he'd say, "Oh, you might burn your hand, Sweetie; let me do it." He treated her as if she were a fragile china doll.

Today George's wife has no sense of value or responsibility, is virtually helpless, and is a chronic alcoholic. George dearly loved his wife, but he encouraged her to become sort of a doll, and a human being must have more meaning than just being a decorative doll. Affirming the wrong things in others can be very destructive.

Punishing Each Other

However, married people more often hurt each other by getting into vicious retaliatory cycles, each one punishing the other for his or her misdeeds.

It is tragic to see so many people who come for counseling after 10 to 20 years of marriage, with great walls of hostility, bitterness, and resentment between them. Commonly, in their egocentricity they see the problem as residing almost exclusively with the other person, and their primary focus is how to make the other person conform to their requirements.

When Paul first came for counseling, it was because he was experiencing attacks in which he thought he was either going to die or lose his mind. He would start breathing fast, sweating, develop a heavy feeling in his chest, rapid pulse, and a feeling that something dreadful was going to happen at any minute.

He had taken tranquilizers off and on but continued to have the attacks. He wondered if there were some help besides taking pills.

Paul's basic problem centered around his relationship with his wife. She was very independent, and had an important career. He felt she neglected the house and put her career first.

On the other hand, she didn't feel loved. She always felt on trial, as if she were being judged. She was never shown affection, and the only time she was touched was when he was interested in a sexual relationship. If she approached him just for affection, he would withdraw.

She tended to punish Paul for his lack of attention or acceptance by not doing things in the home that he wished. He punished her by aloofness, coldness, and criticalness. She began more and more to find her emotional needs met in her work and church. He found his emotional needs met more and more in civic affairs. And they grew further and further apart.

I shared principles with them of how to interrupt such cycles, and they tried to apply them. They often got into trouble by trying to second guess what the other one "really meant," because they were not used to having honest, open communications. They frequently misinterpreted each other, and then more problems arose from that.

However, they did begin to share more honestly and openly, to come closer together, to understand each other better, and to reach out to each other rather than punish the other for not "doing right." Thus they began interrupting some of the self-perpetuating destructive cycles. An important breakthrough came for this couple when Paul became a Christian. This greatly changed his sense of priorities and brought them together as one in this most important area, whereas Christianity had been a source of division between them.

The fact that he became a Christian did not, of course, solve all their problems, but it did give an extremely important base from which to work things out, since he had new motivations, new guidelines, and new capacities.

Ultimately, not only did Paul's distressing attacks cease, but the couple became much happier together, and each of them profited personally from the relationship with the other.

The Communication Gap

In recent years there has been much talk about a generation gap. Some have suggested that much of the gap is in the area of communication. Of course, this is true. What we say or don't say has a powerful influence on the quality of our relationships.

However, it is important to understand that, regardless of the actual content of our words, certain principles are in operation "behind the scenes," as it were.

For example, every time we interact with someone, the quality of the relationship is being established. Underlying questions are being asked, or statements are being made. What do you think of me? Do you care? Am I smarter? Are you stronger? Such issues as these are underneath even the most innocuous sounding questions or statements.

Some people have a profound need of being one up in little subtle ways as a discussion is going on. They are really saying, "I must come off smarter, stronger than you."

I caught myself doing this at a pastors' conference in Tennessee. One of the pastors was presenting concepts I had learned and had been using for some time. My old infantile ego began to react. As we apparently discussed a particular topic, I let him know he wasn't telling me anything I didn't already know. That was old stuff to me, and how could he possibly think otherwise?

What was really going on beneath that communication? I was defining my superior relationship. I was saying, "You're not going to be my instructor, Buddy. I'm the authority around here."

The Doughnut Episode

Often the communication asks and answers the question, *Am I important to you? Am I loved?* I'll never forget one time when my oldest boy came in and asked for a doughnut.

I answered, "Sure, Jim." So he took the doughnut. It happened to be the last one. In a couple of minutes, son #2, who is 11 months younger and often feels outdone by his older brother, came in and asked, "Daddy, can I have a doughnut?"

"Sure, Roger, go ahead."

But there were no more.

"How come I can't have a doughnut?" Roger complained. And then came the universal wail familiar to all parents. "Jim *always* gets everything! I *never* get anything!"

Now if I'd been having a bad day or not listening to what was really being asked, I could have gotten into a tremendous harangue with him about the doughnut. "Well, what am I supposed to do, bake some doughnuts? Can't you see we don't have any? Am I supposed to bring one out of thin air and give it to you?"

I have gotten into this kind of harangue. But on this particular day I was listening, and I realized the issue was not doughnuts. So, I said, "You know, Roger, I love you every bit as much as I love Jim. I wish we had a whole plate of doughnuts so we could sit down and chomp them all up. But we are all out; we don't have any. Let's see what else we can find."

That took care of the issue in 10 seconds. There was no unpleasantness, because I was listening to the basic question. What was the question? It was, "Do you love me as much as you love Jim?" Similarly, questions are being asked about relationships in almost any communication. We must pay attention to these underlying questions and statements about our relationships if we are going to increase understanding and communicate meaningfully.

A Hearing For the Truth

It's also important to realize that no matter what the topic, every communication is, to use a clinical term, either therapeutic or nontherapeutic. Call it constructive or destructive.

Many times our one-upmanship or our self-centeredness or our self-righteousness is such that we are more interested in proving our point, justifying ourselves, making sure the person learned a lesson, than we are in listening to or understanding him. Are we being helpful, or hurtful?

A teen-ager recently told me, "I can never talk to Mother. No matter what I say, she has the nose of a bloodhound to sniff out some issue that requires a sermon. She only listens to find something to preach about."

One of the most important principles that underlies communication is that simply saying what is correct, simply stating truth, is not enough. We have not fulfilled our responsibility as parents, as children, as spouses, or in any other role just by saying what is true. Many people speak truth, but the manner in which they speak it virtually guarantees the truth will not be heard.

Therefore we need to produce an environment where truth can be heard. Often in my office I hear a person say something true to a member of his family. I am convinced that his statement is correct, that it is something the other person really should stop doing or start doing, but the speaker has interacted destructively regardless of the fact that he is telling the truth. He has spoken truth in such a way as to communicate, "I don't respect you," or, "I hate you," or, "You're stupid," or, "You are totally unacceptable to me until you become something else," or, "I am holier than thou."

When these kinds of destructive communications accompany truth, the truth is worthless, because it isn't heard, and nothing constructive takes place.

I like the way the Apostle John describes Jesus Christ as "full of grace and truth" (John 1:14, KJV). Truth without grace can be harsh and cutting, and learning will not take place in that setting. On the other hand, grace without truth can come through as wishy-washy, namby-pamby, 99 shades of gray and compromise. We must both speak the truth and speak it with grace.

We communicate a great deal more than we realize by our voice tones, our posture, our gestures, our facial expressions. I sometimes catch myself getting angry with someone for no apparent reason. Then suddenly I realize that he or she has a pained, puzzled expression as if what I'm saying is either incomprehensible or ridiculous.

I suspect a painful exercise for any family would be to record on tape everything said during one day, then to turn on the playback without paying any attention to the words spoken, and simply listen to the voice tones. They would hear critical voice tones, disgust, rejection, haughtiness, whining. Sometimes we develop these destructive voice tones as a habit and are hardly aware of them.

The noise a wife makes as she works in the kitchen or cleans can communicate a good bit about how she's feeling. A sensitive husband should be aware of this. The way a husband cracks open the newspaper or does some of his chores around the house can tell the wife a good deal if she is listening. You can learn to pay attention to another person's body language—his nonverbal communications.

If you are committed to being a creative interactor, you won't take offense at what you learn, but you will act in such a way that something helpful takes place. The action may involve allowing the person to be alone for a while, or it may involve simply an expression from you that you understand how he feels without making a big deal out of it.

The issue of how to produce an environment or

relationship where truth will be heard is so crucial that I am going to devote a later chapter to it.

Common Blocks to Helpful Communications

Whether between husband and wife, friends, co-workers, or anyone else, communication must have a sense of mutuality. We cannot deal with issues, solve problems, or really communicate on a one-way basis.

Many people complain that someone important to them won't communicate. Unfortunately, they may be actually blocking communication from the other person by some of their own attitudes. Let's look at some of the most common blocks to communication.

Withdrawal

We are all guilty of withdrawal in many different ways. We may simply be silent when a word or two would have been appreciated.

One time our family, on a trip, stopped at a roadside restaurant, and I ordered. Afterward, one of my sons, who was more tuned in to people at the time than I, said, "Daddy, why didn't you ever look at the waitress?" Then I realized I had simply treated her as an object, not as a person.

We can go through day after busy day, around people and yet withdrawn. It takes a discipline and a commitment to develop sensitivity to other people—to their feelings, their needs—and to resist the tendency to retreat within oneself.

Phyllis was a 32-year-old chronically depressed wife. She said, "I always have to interrupt my husband. He seems constantly engrossed in something else."

It turned out that her husband was very fearful

of being controlled by his wife, whom he saw as being demanding. He seemed to feel he had to ward her off, and he did it by withdrawing into ceaseless activity of one kind or another. The more he went his own way and did his own thing, the more fearful she became of abandonment and the more interrupting she became.

Wives frequently describe their husbands' withdrawal techniques in the following terms: "Every time I try to talk to him, he hides behind the newspaper, turns the TV volume up, or just walks out of the room. Or he starts running some electrical motor and can't hear me any more."

While the complaint of withdrawal is heard more frequently from wives than husbands, one man said that every time he tried to talk to his wife she found something to pick up to carry to the laundry room. Her answer to his complaint was, "You don't want the house looking like a trash heap, do you?" I suspect the marriage would have been better off if she had tended less to having the house aseptic and listened more to her husband.

Another method of withdrawal is simply to change the topic and not deal with the issue at hand. One time in group therapy a woman with a black eye was complaining how cruel her husband was. When the group finally got to the bottom of it, they were less than sympathetic. It seems she had asked him if he had remembered to take out the garbage while they were in the midst of making love.

Or perhaps it's one of those golden moments when the husband is actually sharing something important to him. Possibly the wife listens for a while; then she remembers, "Oh, we forgot to pay the water bill yesterday!" That's the end of his communication, and she wonders why he "never talks."

Many marriages apparently operate successfully on a mutual withdrawal basis. There is no open warfare; all is calm and peaceful. Each may be afraid to say anything that matters, because they are afraid it will upset the peaceful coexistence. They have opted for a mutual disarmament life-style.

While all is peaceful on the surface, this type of marriage relationship often cannot withstand crisis. The couple may go along in this fashion for a long period of time, but all the while the husband and wife are drifting further and further apart. This can be the type situation over which everyone is astounded. The husband and wife, who have had a "perfect" marriage for 10 to 25 years, suddenly find the marriage utterly devastated, and one or the other has taken up with someone else. "But they never had a cross word; they never had any problems," people say.

Building a relationship takes hard-nosed loving, taking risks, reaching out, and working through problems. This will not take place with coexistence, peaceful or otherwise. In this setting, neither is really relating to the other. No one is hearing, and they drift further and further apart. Then when stress comes in the form of a temptation, or some severe problem, they fall apart, because there's no strength to that kind of relationship.

Why do we withdraw? Why are we so afraid to be close to others? The biggest reason we withdraw is that we are afraid of being hurt, or judged, or rejected.

Of course there are times when temporary withdrawal is the wisest action to take. Sometimes in the heat of the moment, speaking off the top of our heads, we say very hurtful, destructive things. The problem with "temporary withdrawal" is that it sometimes becomes like "temporary taxes" which persist indefinitely. Continual withdrawal is death to communication, and noncommunication is death to a good relationship.

Disallowance of Feeling

Often when someone expresses a feeling, the other person's response is, "Oh, you shouldn't feel that way." Or, "How can you feel that way?" Or, "It's stupid for you to feel that way." There's only one thing wrong—the person *does* feel that way.

This disallowance of feeling, just because you don't happen to agree, is a very common block in communication. When you shoot back: "It's dumb to feel that way," or "How can you feel that way?" you are in fact hitting at the very core of the person. It represents a denunciation or belittlement. Rightly or wrongly the person has those feelings. They are a part of him. Disallowing feelings is a deep rejection of the person himself. Instead, we should try to understand the person's feelings. This encourages communication and assists us to be helpful.

Sometimes mothers and fathers disallow the feelings of their children. The child comes in crying over something that to an adult is ridiculous. He dropped his sucker on the ground, and the ants got all over it. So what's the big deal? We tell the child, "Oh, don't feel like that. Don't be a crybaby." But the child does feel like that. Disallowing feelings is hurtful; it drives wedges between husbands and wives, between parents and children.

We ought to react just the opposite way. When

anybody expresses a feeling, that is the time we ought to be the most sensitive, the most attentive, the most accepting, the most involved. We might say to the child who has suffered the contamination of his sucker, "Oh, that's too bad, but, it's all right; we can wash that sucker as good as new!" Of course, some situations cannot be so easily remedied but we can still listen and empathize. This encourages more communication, while disallowance of feeling is almost sure to make the person hesitate to confide in us again.

Defensiveness

Another tremendous block in communication is defensiveness. Your spouse opens up and mentions something you do that really bugs him or her, and you start getting defensive.

Wife: "What, you're going to a meeting again tonight? You're *never* home any more!"

Husband: "What do you mean, I'm never home? I was home on a Tuesday evening only a week or so ago!"

Because he is reacting defensively, the husband has not really responded to what his wife was saying. In fact, he didn't even hear what she was saying. She did not mean he was literally never home. She meant that she felt neglected and lonely and would like for him to be home more, or at least to give her some assurance that she matters to him and that he would like to spend some time with her. Since he has heard none of that, he answers her obviously illogical statement with cruel male "logic."

The trouble with being defensive is that it never deals with the problem. Get defensive and the possibility of any meaningful communication taking place is absolutely zero—guaranteed. You can kiss helpful communication good-bye, because what you have communicated to the other person is, *"It's really your problem.* It's not my problem, and furthermore I'm not going to do anything about it."

And what is the other person's reaction when you get defensive? Often it is, "Well, he didn't hear me. He's not getting the message. So what I have to do is come on stronger." And the stronger he or she comes on, the more defensive you get. And communication goes right out the window.

The Counterattack

A hostile variation of the defensive block is the counterattack.

Wife: "I'm just so tired of picking up after you. Your clothes are all over the place; you leave your towels on the floor. It looks like a strip-tease artist has tramped through here."

Husband: "Well, you are not the cleanest person in the world yourself. Every time I open the kitchen cabinets, something spills out, and you've got so much lingerie hanging around in the bathroom it looks like a jungle in there. You've got a lot of nerve to say anything about me."

The counterattack never solves problems. Rather than dealing with the issue, the other person brings up a different issue. I see many couples in my office whose communication patterns are typically like this. Nothing is ever resolved. One says one thing, and then the other hurls something else back at them. The conversation leaps from one hostile area to another, without any resolution.

Either person could prevent this type of destructive interaction. In the example above, the wife could have expressed her feelings without sounding so accusatory and guilt-provoking. Her approach only increased the chances of her husband responding defensively or with the counterattack. The husband, on the other hand, instead of going on an ego trip, could have recognized his wife's frustration in dealing with a never ending thankless task. He could have communicated his awareness of her feelings and committed himself to doing something about it.

Super-Guilt

Provoking guilt is one of the more destructive blocks in communication. A subtle and usually dishonest method of provoking guilt is to totally collapse and be crushed by some complaint. "Oh, it's all my fault; I'm just so horrible. I don't know how you put up with me. I'm the worst mother (husband, wife) in the world."

The one who issued the complaint is now supposed to feel like a wretch for causing such anguish, and certainly can't push the case any further. Meanwhile the person at fault is saying in effect, "If I suffer enough, and if I'm guilty enough, somehow this will compensate. In other words, I don't have to change my behavior any; I just have to feel guilty."

Alfred Adler, one of the first psychiatrists to break with Sigmund Freud, made this interesting statement: "Those who feel guilty have no intention of changing." There is a powerful core of truth to this, because if you have seen what the problem is and you are going to change and do something about it, there's no need to feel guilty. So heaping guilt on ourselves is often a way of trying to control the other person by causing him to feel guilty.

Of course, sometimes our guilt provocations are

very direct. "You're killing your mother."/"Every gray hair on my head is because of you."/"I've worked myself to death and this is the thanks I get."

Controlling by guilt is an automatic reflex with some people. They operate on the assumption: "If I make them feel guilty, they will do what I want them to do." But this technique always backfires; it produces frustration, irritation, and anger.

David was a young man separated from his wife. I asked him, "What is the first thing that comes to your mind as a reason you would not want to go back with her?" It turned out that when he would want to go fishing occasionally on Saturdays, she would heap guilt upon him. She would throw at him the charge that he was deserting her and was never with her.

That provocation of guilt was the thing that came to David's mind first. Granted, it may not really have been the biggest issue, but this was the first emotionally charged reaction he had to his wife.

Provoking guilt may seem to work for a while as a control mechanism, but it is a destructive and neurotic practice that destroys communication.

Peace at Any Price
Some people contribute to the breakdown in communication for what on the surface seem to be very fine reasons. "My husband has enough burdens in his work without my telling him about this." / "My wife worries enough, without my adding to her concerns." / "Why share this with him; he can't do anything about it." / "I just don't want to cause any trouble."

People often try to keep peace by refusing to

deal with problems. Then when more problems are collected than they can handle, they finally come bursting to the surface in such a way that more harm is done than if they had been dealt with along the way.

Jill married at 16, and by the time she was in her mid 20s had four children. Though there was a great deal of unhappiness in their relationships, she and her husband never would get down to brass tacks to talk about their basic problems. They just let things build up more and more.

After a surgical operation, Jill felt she couldn't stand the warfare any more. She became agitated, irrational, and decided to go off with some man she cared little about. She thought better of it, however, and soon returned. Her having been away for just a matter of hours provoked a crisis which forced her husband to sit down and talk with her.

With her husband willing to listen and with Jill at last talking about their real problems, the immediate crisis was relieved and the basis for a more satisfactory relationship through communication was established.

Our reasons for not getting things out in the open may seem good, but communication is necessary. What is not out in the open cannot really be dealt with and cannot be healed, and as we go underground with feelings, we usually can expect negative results.

But let's go on to better things. It's important to recognize what we are doing to each other . . . and how. Just understanding some of the pitfalls discussed in this chapter—and avoiding them—can help your relationships immensely.

But there is more—much more—that we can do

for each other. And, indirectly, for ourselves. For what husband or wife wants to live with an unhappy partner? Or who wants to be plagued with enemies and unnecessary grief? The way out of needless and harmful conflict lies, first of all, through understanding who we are as humans. It is that understanding we will seek now.

Part II

Who Are We?

2

This Creature Called Man

Few individuals in human history have been more favored with natural gifts than Johann Chrysostomus Wolfgang Amadeus Mozart. At age five he wrote an advanced concerto for the harpsichord. At seven, he was performing the most difficult compositions of Bach and Handel. At 14, he composed his first opera.

Yet, this "best pianist and greatest composer of his time—perhaps of all history"—died in poverty and obscurity at age 35. His widow was ill and seemed indifferent to his burial. A few friends went as far as the church but were deterred by a storm from going to the grave. By the time anyone bothered to inquire about it, the location of the grave was impossible to discover. Mozart's unmarked grave became lost for all time.

History has recorded many cases of great men and women who went unrecognized and unacknowledged in their time.

Then, there are the not-so-great. In Cairo, Egypt, two families shared the same water pump. When it needed repair, a quarrel arose over who was going to pay the bill. One thing led to another until bullets began to fly. When it was all over, a total of 18 people were dead. The repair bill on the pump was 55¢. That figures out to just slightly over three cents per human life.

What is a human really worth? Obviously, sometimes, in the eyes of other people, not very much.

Nor is a man always worth much in his own eyes. To a 17-year-old boy in Waukesha, Wis., life was worthless without a car to drive. After losing his driver's license, he wrote a note saying, "Without a license I don't have my car, job, or social life. So I think that it is better to end it all right now." Then he fired a bullet through his head.

But the Bible teaches that man has great worth. Every man, regardless of race, social status, intelligence, or any other quality, is important by virtue of the fact that he is made "in the image of God."

Thus the Psalmist writes, "When I look up into the night skies and see the work of Your fingers— the moon and the stars You have made—I cannot understand how You can bother with mere puny man, to pay any attention to him! And yet You have made him only a little lower than the angels and placed a crown of glory and honor on his head. You have put him in charge of everything You made; everything is put under his authority" (Ps. 8:3-6).

So important to psychological health is the concept of self-worth that I am dealing with it at length in a subsequent chapter of this book. At this juncture, my purpose is to point out that the *only adequate and valid base* for a concept of self-worth must be found in the fact that man is created in the image of God. Any other basis for understanding man reduces him to so much meaningless machinery in a universe that developed by chance.

A number of other human characteristics cannot be understood or explained on any other basis than man being created in the image of God. A person can never understand why he behaves as he does, nor the importance and implications of his behavior, until he understands who and what he is. Two basic truths about man—every man—must be reckoned with, or we wander in darkness wondering why we stumble.

Since this understanding is so basic and crucial to human behavior, we must take pains to grasp it clearly. Otherwise, we are not facing reality.

Man Bears the Image of God

Profound words about the essential nature of man leap out at us from the opening pages of the Bible. "Then God said, 'Let Us make a man—someone like Ourselves, to be the master of all life upon the earth and in the skies and in the seas.' So God made man like his Maker. Like God did God make man; man and maid did He make them. And God blessed them and told them, 'Multiply and fill the earth and subdue it; you are masters of the fish and birds and all the animals'" (Gen. 1:26-28). Or as it says in the very familiar King James Version, "God created man in His own image" (Gen. 1:27). No culture has been found on the face of the earth that was not drawn toward the concept of God. It may be a terribly distorted concept but nevertheless it exists.

Consider what it means to say that we are in His image or that we are a "shadow" of Him. Obviously, it has nothing whatsoever to do with physical characteristics. Jesus told the Samaritan woman at the well that those who worship God must worship Him in spirit and in truth, for *God is a spirit* (John 4:24, KJV). Our likeness to God is not physical; it has to do with the qualities of God. The qualities of God revealed in Scripture include His creativeness, the fact that He is a God who communicates, loves, is absolutely just, makes choices, and has purpose and meaning behind His choices.

Because man is in the image of God, he has built-in needs to be creative, communicative, to love, to be just, to be free to make choices, and to experience meaning in his life. We are the only creatures on earth that have these needs.

A Drive Within

Our needs as humans can never be fully realized unless we are rightly related to God, to ourselves, and to our fellow men. We have a drive within ourselves to reach out to satisfy these needs as surely as a seedling plant reaches for the sun. And we will be frustrated and unfulfilled if we order our lives totally around an animalistic or materialistic existence.

Granted, some people don't *seem* to have these spiritual needs. They seem only concerned about gratifying the animal instincts for food, sex, and shelter. But this indifference to spiritual values is more apparent than real.

It may be a cynical surrender to animal living resulting from the disillusionment of previous failure in reaching after higher things. It may be the expression of a life-style that seems perfectly logical based on the philosophy of the day that depicts man as only an animal who has developed by chance, without meaning, but with instincts that must be gratified as he feels them. People who try to order their lives around such a philosophy become driven, restless, bored, or despairing. They are not functioning as they were designed.

When you see a person living like an animal, you may be sure this is also a person who does not understand *who he is,* a creature with the unique honor of having been created in God's image.

John Bunyan depicts such people under the image of the man with the muckrake. Here is a stooped figure of a man, preoccupied with raking through the muck and mire at his feet so that he might perhaps find a morsel to sustain life or a trinket to brighten it. All the time, poised over his head is a glittering crown, the symbol of a nobler life for which he was intended. But he never sees the crown because he's too busy raking the muck.

This is a picture of many, many people. But though they may not have even an inkling of what they lack, and no consciousness at all of aspirations after God, they are discontented, fragmented, incomplete. Made in the image of God, they never have escaped and never can quite escape the implications of that fact.

Man Is Supremely Self-Centered

When we understand that we are created only a little lower than the angels, greatly loved by God, given tremendous qualities that no other creatures possess, and designed for rulership, we still have only one side of the picture. We need more insight to understand fully who we are, and this involves knowing the true nature of sin.

A story tells of a preacher who announced he had made an exhaustive study of sin and had identified and catalogued every sin in existence. His list, which he waved before the eyes of the audience, included 86 commonly known and obscure sins.

Afterward, the preacher was besieged with requests for the list by people from the audience who were afraid they might have missed out on something!

Actually, it was that very appeal that lured Eve into eating the forbidden fruit. She was afraid she was missing out on something.

The biblical description of the first sin is a model of the problem that we all face. How did Satan seduce Eve? He appealed to her self-interest. He persuaded her to assert her will against the will of God. He did it through her desire to be wise as God. Satan said, in effect, "You know, the reason God doesn't want you to eat this fruit is because you'll be as smart as He is. See, God is mean; He wants to deprive you of something desirable."

Of course, since God is good and is perfect love, He denied Adam and Eve nothing that was really good, but Satan, the deceiver, made an offer the pair could hardly resist; it sounded so good.

A New Zealand publication carried an intriguing advertisement of a "tested and proved" method for cutting household bills in half. It offered prospective customers the opportunity to get in on the secret for only $3. How could the promoters guarantee such fantastic results? That was what the police wanted to know. They found that the advertisers planned to send each customer a cheap pair of scissors.

This kind of deception is suggestive of the way Satan deceived Eve. He offered her fabulous benefits: to be like God, knowing good and evil. And he kept his promise in the sense that Eve did come to know firsthand what evil was all about. And its basic nature was in Eve's choice to go her own way and choose her own will rather than God's will. Eve chose the route of egocentricity, as, of course, did Adam, though he perhaps did it more deliberately (see 1 Tim. 2:14).

Now, this is what sin is all about. People often focus on sin, meaning bad behavior, as man's basic problem. But man's basic problem is self-worship, self-centeredness, egocentricity, whatever word you want to use for the big "I" in the middle of sin. It is the big "I" that has led man away from God and into paths of his own choosing.

God in a Hole

A few years ago a young American named Bruce Olson risked and almost lost his life to reach the uncivilized Motilone Indians of South America with the Gospel of Christ. After he had lived among the Motilones about three years and had learned enough of their language and customs to communicate with them, he found he had an unexpected problem.

The Motilones were too good! They did not steal from one another. Marital infidelity was unknown among them. They did not even squabble among themselves, but lived, seemingly, in delightful harmony. And they did not drink or smoke.

How could Olson preach about sin and salvation to such a people? To those who far surpassed the people of "Christian America" in morality?

Then, one day, Olson came across a Motilone in the jungle who was crying out and calling into a large rectangular hole in the ground. The man was calling on God.

As Olson asked questions, he learned that the Motilones believed they had once known God. But a deceiver had come, and promising to lead them to a better hunting ground had, instead, led them away from God.

Here was Olson's enlightenment. Moral as they were, the Motilones did not know God, and they realized it. Because they were created in the image of God, they had the need to know Him personally, to experience life at a more fulfilled level by having God Himself indwell them. Olson presented Christ to them as the One who "once suffered for sins, the just for the unjust, that He might *bring us to God*" (1 Peter 3:18, KJV). Today, he estimates that 90% of the Motilones have trusted Christ and found completion and fulfillment in Him.

A commonly held and rather naive view is that a man is a sinner because he practices certain behavior that God or society happens to define as wrong. Not so. Man is a sinner because of his basic condition of self-centeredness.

From infancy on, we tend to position ourselves in the center of our universe and demand that everything revolve around us, catering to our needs and desires. The infant is very direct: screaming, hollering, kicking. As we become adults, we are much more subtle and may be very clever with our words, but the same kicking, screaming infant is still within. Were we to verbalize this attitude, we would say something like this: "I want to run *my* life on *my* terms, and I don't want anybody, including God, telling me otherwise."

So, we eat the forbidden fruit, because we want to.

We leave God to find a better hunting ground, because we want to.

Put it in the terms of your own culture, your own personal life. However you may have expressed it, the basic fact of your life is that you have gone your own way.

Haven't you?

Of course, this is nothing less than idolatry. It is a case of self-worship. We put ourselves in the place of God. And we violate the first and greatest commandment which is to "love the Lord thy God with all thy heart and with all thy soul and with all thy mind" (Matt. 22:37, KJV). We reserve that kind of devotion for ourselves alone!

Every Man's Battle

This leads us into inevitable and intense conflict, because this egocentricity plays against the innate image of God residing within us. The Godlike qualities of creativity, communication, love, justice, choice, and purpose are constantly being frustrated by our egocentricity, so that we are automatically in conflict. We don't have to go out and do something that some court of law may call wrong or some church group may call sin. Just by virtue of our position, regardless of what we do, we're caught up in this conflict.

"When I want to do good, I don't; and when I try not to do wrong, I do it anyway. Now, if I am doing what I don't want to, it is plain where the trouble is: sin still has me in its evil grasp" (Rom. 7:19, 20).

Someone says, "Hold on, now. That Scripture is talking about the *Christian* and the conflict that exists between his old, sinful nature and the new nature of Christ within him."

True. But the old sinful nature is his egocentricity. And the new nature of Christ within also brings about a renewing of the image of God in a man, an image which, as we have seen, was never totally obliterated.

In both cases, Christian or not, there is conflict between man's image-of-God characteristics and his egocentricity. The conflict may and often does *intensify* when a person becomes a Christian, for the image of God is renewed in him. But along with increased conflict, there is a new element present for the Christian. The Holy Spirit now indwells us and begins to direct us in reaching our rightful destiny, which is to be conformed to the image of Jesus Christ (Rom. 8:29). As we grow, our being created in the image of God is less and less handicapped by egocentricity, and we can become more fulfilled and experience more victory in conflict.

So what does the Apostle Paul say, in effect? "I love to do God's will so far as my new nature is concerned. But there is something else deep within me, in my lower nature, that is at war with my mind and wins the fight and makes me a slave to the sin that is still within me. In my mind I want to be God's willing servant, but instead I find myself still enslaved to sin. . . . My new life tells me to do right, but the old nature that is still inside me loves to sin. Oh, what a terrible predicament I am in! Who will free me from my slavery?" (Rom. 7:22-24)

But, see, the good news is that we don't have to stay stuck in this conflict, and that's Paul's very next statement. "Who will free me from my slavery to this deadly lower nature? Thank God! It has been done by Jesus Christ our Lord. He has set me free" (Rom. 7:24, 25).

Paul is describing—much more honestly than the average church member ever does—the conflict resulting from the basic self-centeredness still within him. But he doesn't have to stay stuck there, because, as he lives as a Christian, the power of

Jesus Christ within him gives him the possibility of victory in this conflict.

The Great Design

Now, we are here talking about something quite different from merely adding a religious dimension to one's life. We are talking about Jesus Christ Himself indwelling us through the power of the Holy Spirit. Religion itself can be egocentric, as it was with the Pharisees of Jesus' day who used prayer and all their religious observances in a self-righteous way to commend themselves to God. Religion can be so much window dressing, to conceal just how totally egocentric a person is.

Others who admit God into their thinking may do so in a shallow and inadequate way. This is the reason the Bible is so critically important, because it tells us of the true nature of God and man and how we are designed to function. One of the inadequate views of the Bible is that it gives some select dos and don'ts that one tries to follow in order to be a good person. But it's so much deeper than that.

God is telling us, "I created you; I created the universe. I know all about you—what your thoughts are going to be before you think them. I love you and I'm concerned about you. And I'm going to let you in on reality. I'm going to let you in on the nature of the universe I created. And I'm going to let you in on the kind of relationships that work between husbands and wives, between parents and children, and between you and Me, and on how you can begin to grow toward your rightful destiny—becoming a real man or woman as I intended."

Unfortunately, many people try to conduct their

lives as if the Bible were not true, or they are ignorant of some of the Bible's important principles. And they get into difficulties as surely as will a little child who doesn't understand the principle that when something is glowing red it's likely to be hot and injurious.

Our need, you see, is to live in God's universe as He created it. Those who try to live as if these principles were not true will certainly pay the consequences for it.

More Light

So let us ask, what else does the Bible say about the nature of man? Isaiah 53:6 gives a clear statement of this whole problem of our wanting to do things our way. "We are the ones who strayed away like sheep! We, who left God's paths to follow our own." See, that's the basic sin; we want to put self first and go on our own path, our own route, our own way. All sin stems from this basic position.

Romans 3:23 says *all*—everybody in the universe —"have sinned and come short of the glory of God" (KJV). We have come short of the glory that God created us for and basically meant us to exhibit. We have come short of that because we have gone off on our egocentric route. That's why there is inevitable conflict for every human being.

Now, some people have denied God so long and have turned their back on Him so long that the rudiments of their Godlikeness would be very hard to find. They have become more and more like animals and less and less like God (see Rom. 1: 18-32). Their only hope is to be born again, remade in God's image. This incredible renewal occurs when one receives Jesus Christ into his life!

That, you see, is one reason receiving Jesus

Christ becomes so very important, and this is one of the unique distinctives of Christianity. There are other religions that have very fine ethics, but they don't deal with the problem of the basic nature of man. They have these myths that if you go through the six steps of this or the eight steps of that, you finally will have some kind of peaceful relationship with God. But what's needed is a *radical internal* change that deals with our egocentricity, that restores the image of God in us. There is nothing we can do about this simply by trying to change our behavior or actions.

The Divine Exchange

The reason that the Cross is so dominant in Christianity is that God chose this method to reveal how a radical change in us is possible. "For God took the sinless Christ and poured into Him our sins. Then, in exchange, He poured God's goodness into us!" (2 Cor. 5:21) Only this "exchange" can bring us into a new life with new capacities and motivations.

Jesus Christ took within His own being the estrangement, the guilt-provoking sin of egocentricity, and carried it to His grave. Then, on the third day, He rose again triumphant over sin and death. It is His Spirit who will indwell, and bring the beginning of new life to, the person who will admit his sin, his need, and receive the cleansing and forgiveness God wants us to have.

Can you picture the enormity of this "exchange," and what it cost God? Here is the Son of God, tempted in all points like as we, human yet God, who then has flooding into His very being all of this egocentricity, the basic sin, the big I. This was the agony, and this is what separated Him from God.

That's why He cried out, "My God, My God, why hast Thou forsaken Me?" (Mark 15:34, KJV) He was forsaken. God cannot have fellowship with this egocentricity.

We have learned, then, who we are by *creation*: individuals made in the image of God. We also have explored who we can be by *redemption*: beneficiaries of the cross of Christ, who have experienced the glorious "exchange" whereby our sins are put to His account and His righteousness to ours.

Sometimes as Christians try to communicate these powerful truths, they are accused of being like Victor Borge's uncle, who was said to have found a cure for which there was no disease. Many people simply do not understand that they are created in the image of God, and that the reason they are in such desperate straits with no meaning to life, no purpose, no guidelines is that they have not dealt with their egocentricity problem and are not functioning as God designed them. All they can do is their "own thing" and hope it turns out. And it doesn't.

But this is what makes Christianity so exciting and so necessary and why it is not a cure for which there is no disease, because it's the cure for the disease that every human being in the world has— this problem of self-centeredness that brings all men into conflict with the image-of-God aspect of their being.

The person who has recognized his egocentricity and has wanted to turn away from it (repent) and ask Jesus Christ to come into his life and lead him, finds exciting new possibilities for victory in the conflict. Not that the conflict disappears. That's a myth. Any teaching that would have you think that when you become a Christian, it's all peace and joy, is neurotic, and not related to reality. That's not the way it is. But we do have a new power within to gain more and more freedom from self-centeredness. In other words, the battle continues, but now the defeats are reduced and the victories increased. And that difference has tremendous and almost limitless implications for a better life.

Some of these implications will be spelled out in the succeeding chapters of this book.

3

"Get the Cheerios Off My Chair"

Picture this. I come home from work. My wife has been at home all day and, of course, she hasn't had much to do. She has cleaned the house three times. The dog has had a violent gastrointestinal disorder in the living room. My scientific-minded son has put the cat in the refrigerator to see if all that thick, hairy fur will keep him warm. My wife has arbitrated differences presented with great emotion to her by our four children, and on occasion clobbered an offender. Supper is ready on time by great effort on her part, and I come home, barely grunt a greeting, sit down at the table, and say, "Why are there Cheerios stuck to the seat of my chair?"

Now my wife is vulnerable at this point! She is likely to become defensive, and instead of dealing with my discomfort at having Cheerios on my chair, she may begin to talk about all the work she's done that day. Which is fine, but it doesn't remove the offending cereal.

At this point, some reader is sure to say, "What a male chauvinist! Get the Cheerios off of your own dumb chair. I sure feel sorry for your wife."

OK, and maybe in that situation, my wife would also feel sorry for herself! In which case, she might not just be defensive, as I've described above. She might go on the counterattack. "You have some nerve complaining about the Cheerios on your chair, the way you leave your shoes scattered all over the entire house! And furthermore. . . ."

Great. Now I not only have Cheerios stuck to my chair, but I have a fight with my wife on my hands. However justified my wife's defensiveness or counterattack may seem, neither reaction on her part helps the situation.

Both reactions are among the blocks to constructive communications, which we discussed in chapter one.

What then, *should* my wife do in this situation? She should understand *who she is as a Christian* and cope with the problem on a spiritual level.

It may sound absurd, to talk of dealing with so trivial a matter on a spiritual level. However, let me assure you that much emotional energy can be consumed over trivial matters, and relationships between people very often fail or succeed in just such seemingly insignificant circumstances.

You must understand what I mean when I speak of dealing with such problems on a spiritual level, as a Christian.

An Object of Satan's Attacks

An acquaintance of mine said to me one day, "Would you get into the ring with Muhammad Ali?"

I didn't know what my friend was up to, and the question seemed to cast doubt on my intelligence. The negative answer seemed obvious.

He said, "Well, have you ever stopped to think that there is in fact only one reason that you might get into the ring with Muhammad Ali. That would be if you thought you had a chance to win, if you imagined you were some kind of a match for him. Have you ever considered how powerful Satan must be to have dared war against God? Satan is an intelligent being, and he must have thought he had a chance to win."

Somehow that impressed me, and I understood better the awesomeness of Satan's power. Many Christians are naive about this destructive enemy who would put us down, who would attack us where we are vulnerable and defeat us.

Satan is no fool. Naturally, he will not attack us at our strong points. Like any wily adversary, he studies us, seeking to discover our weak points, the areas where he will have the greatest opportunity for success. However, we cannot say, "The devil made me do it," because we are responsible for our vulnerable areas. We can either give ground to Satan, or we can resist him. The choice, and the responsibility, is ours.

In the case of my wife, she is vulnerable in the area of feeling inadequate as a mother and home-maker. And, of course, she doesn't like to have an insensitive husband grumble about Cheerios on his chair when she has had a formidable day already.

My complaint not only fails totally to appreciate what she's been through that day, but it implies criticism of her efficiency as a homemaker. She is likely to feel attacked, criticized, put down. Her ego and self-respect are at stake. Obviously, all this is not articulated, but the implications are unmistakably present.

Satan, then, will attack at this vulnerable point.

And she urgently needs to recognize that this is exactly what is happening. Her primary problem is not with the *circumstance* (in this case an insensitive husband). Her primary problem is how she *responds* to the circumstance, whether she appropriates the power of Jesus Christ in resisting Satan and bringing healing into the relationship, or whether she gives in to the satanic pull and converts the incident into an "international crisis."

This trivial incident does involve her in spiritual warfare, as the Bible makes clear. "For we wrestle not against flesh and blood (insensitive husbands, unreasonable wives, unfair superiors), but against principalities, against powers, against the rulers of the darkness of this world, against spiritual wickedness in high places" (Eph. 6:12, KJV). Or, as the preceding verse says, we must "stand against the wiles *of the devil.*"

An Identity as Children of God

The ironic thing about our frequent defeats at the hands of Satan is that they are so unnecessary. We have the superior power on our side! Though we are fighting a tremendously powerful enemy, *he has already been defeated!*

"Greater is He [Jesus Christ] that is in you than he [Satan] that is in the world" (1 John 4:4, KJV). Not only can we defeat Satan through the superior power of Christ, but according to the Apostle Paul we can be "*more* than conquerors through Him that loved us" (Rom. 8:37, KJV).

But *how* can we be more than conquerors? A big part of the secret is in really understanding who we are as Christians. The Apostle Paul confronted Christians at Ephesus and other places saying in effect: "You people don't realize who you are. At one time you were aliens, strangers without the camp. You had no hope; you didn't know where you were going. You didn't know what life was all about. But now, here you are right in the middle of the most majestic miracle of the universe!

"The Lord had a plan before the foundations of the universe were even formed. The prophets wanted to see it and they had only a glimmer of it, but it has been revealed to *you!* God has invaded this planet in the person of Jesus Christ, and He has brought salvation to you. Don't you know that you are part of the family of God? That's right, *you,* a joint heir with Christ! This is *who you are.* Put on this new man—don't go around beaten down by your own infantile egos. Identify yourself!" (See Eph. 2:11—3:6.)

We need to identify ourselves like this every single day. We walk around as if we didn't have this glorious identity. Who are you? Are you a joint heir with Christ? Are you born of God? Are you part of His priesthood?

So we need to understand and affirm who we are as Christians, to commit ourselves minute by minute, hour by hour to Christ, to claim our identity in Him and resist Satan. If something comes up that puts pressure on us in some vulnerable point, instead of coming back with an automatic emotional reaction, we need to identify ourselves as Christians and to recognize Satan's attack.

Now let's go back to the Cheerios and the chair. My wife is vulnerable to feeling that I imply she is not efficient. I put her down. (Of course, what I'm doing is building up my own ego at her expense.) Now suppose that when I lay this Cheerios triviality on her after she's had a pretty awesome day, she realizes that the circumstance of having an unreasonable husband exposes her to the possibility of satanic attack in this vulnerable area. What does she do?

She identifies who she is in Christ—a worthwhile, redeemed child of God. She asks for Satan to be bound in the name of the Lord Jesus Christ. She denies domination to the feeling that she is not understood and not appreciated. Having cast that out in the name of the Lord Jesus Christ, she puts herself into action. She comes over and gives me a kiss and says, "I'm sorry there are Cheerios in the chair." She gets them out.

Now what about *my* attitude? If I'd been living Jesus Christ when I walked through my front door, I'd have noticed the house. I'd have asked her how things are, and I'd have let her know I appreciate her and that I love her. I'd have said nothing about the Cheerios, but picked them out of the chair myself.

Note carefully that either one of us living Christ could bring a redemptive dimension to the situation. And both of us living Christ would bring a truly divine harmony. Instead of having a little bitter undercurrent in our relationship, we would have a new affirmation of love. This is putting Christianity into action. This is what it is all about.

More Than Salvation

If we're going to have this kind of victory, we are going to have to identify who we are, be intelligent about the warfare we are fighting, and actively, moment by moment, resist Satan, claim Jesus Christ, and act creatively, going exactly counter to the little push that Satan would give us.

We are now talking about something quite different from the initial salvation experience. This is one of the problems of the evangelical and conservative groups of which I am a member: we have emphasized the concept of salvation, which needs to be emphasized, but all too often we've neglected to teach people how to live the Christ life. It is as if once a person becomes a Christian, we say, "You're OK. Now we'll deal with this other person who isn't a Christian yet. We have to work on him."

And yet a most exciting, most important, and ultimately a most evangelistic enterprise, would be to help Christians grow and develop in such a way that they would live the kind of life that would make people say, "Hey, you've got something that I need and want!"

In other words, we need Jesus Christ not only for eternal salvation, but also to enable us to live adequately and happily here and now. Many Christians know they are saved by grace, but they have forgotten or never realized that they are to live by grace. The Scriptures tell us that Christ created the world, and He sustains the world, and *He upholds us.* Our job is to be honest about ourselves, to be aware of our enemy Satan, to face the fact that we have a strong drive to go our own route, and most important, to turn ourselves over to Him continually as an ongoing life style. This is not some past-tense deal, or just something we do when we become Christians. Our job is to live in grace and to keep turning our lives over to Him instead of simply being reactors, responding to a stimulus like an animal, and opening the door to Satan. We are to bring something new into action, the creative, healing power of Jesus Christ which is ours through the Holy Spirit who indwells and desires to fill us.

But in order to have this type of victory, a basic and genuine commitment to Jesus Christ must come first, and then we must live it minute by minute. If we don't have this kind of commitment to Jesus Christ, we will *hear* principles that we agree with, but we won't *live* them. We will say, "Yes, that's right. That's the way we ought to live. That's the way a husband ought to treat his wife; that's the way a wife ought to treat her husband." And we will continue to bite and devour one another.

These principles that I am sharing with you do not come naturally. They go against the grain of human nature, as it were. The natural thing to do when someone attacks you is to let him have it, just as hard. These principles will only be nice sounding Sunday School theories unless the dynamic of a genuine commitment to Jesus Christ backs them up and gives you a way of putting them into practice.

Who We Are Corporately

Just as many Christians are insufficiently aware of the power and subtlety of our adversary, Satan, they are also unaware of the tremendous power, rights, privileges, and responsibilities we have corporately. That is, as the body of Christ. We have seen, in the previous chapter, who we are by *creation* and who we can be by *redemption*. Our identity is incomplete, however, until we discover who we are by *corporation*, functioning within the body of Christ.

Jesus asserted in Matthew 18:19, 20 that if two Christians agree here on earth concerning anything they ask, His Father in heaven will do it. Then He goes on to say, "For where two or three gather together because they are Mine, I will be right there among them." He also sent the disciples out two by two. We are not alone as Christians; we have each other.

"Just as there are many parts to our bodies, so it is with Christ's body. We are all parts of it, and it takes every one of us to make it complete, for we each have different work to do. So we belong to each other, and each needs all the others" (Rom. 12:4, 5).

"Now here is what I'm trying to say: All of you together are the one body of Christ, and each one of you is a separate and necessary part of it" (1 Cor. 12:27).

As members of the body of Christ, we are told to restore in a spirit of gentleness anyone who makes a mistake. We are told to bear each other's burdens, confess our sins to each other, pray for each other, work to the interest of others, encourage each other, build each other up, exhort each other, admonish the idle, encourage the faint hearted, help the weak, be patient with all, and do good to one another. We are to forgive each other, and let love be the greatest guide of our relationship with each other. (See Gal. 6:1-3; Phil. 2:1-4; 1 Thes. 5:11, 14-19; Col. 3:12-14.)

We are told to walk in the light as Jesus Christ is in the light. This means to follow Jesus in obedience and to be honest and open. And then, the Scripture goes on to say, "We have fellowship one with another and the blood of Jesus Christ, His Son cleanseth us from all sin" (1 John 1:7, KJV).

For the body to be in ideal health, all of its members must function as they were designed to function. Christians have different gifts, different strengths and weaknesses. Every Christian, as part of the body of Christ, has a particular role to play. If he is to reach his maximum potential, he should be part of a circle of Christian friends who can teach each other, confront each other, support each other, challenge each other, and pray for each other.

Often Christians are too busy passing judgment on each other to have this kind of fellowship. One great failing that seems to be part of human nature is to think that everyone should have exactly the same kind of experience we have had and use the same kind of phrases we use to describe it.

Some Christians have a very divisive effect on the body of Christ because they think everybody should be mouth or feet or hands. They have failed to grasp the concept that Christians have *different* gifts. We are different members of the body, and it takes all working together for the body to function as it should.

Many Christians are prone to go on an ego trip and think only their group has had the right experience or is true to the Scripture or expresses worship properly. Some of the greatest attacks on Christ's Church come from Christians who are walking after the flesh and not the Spirit, who in their pride and conceit think they have some sort of monopoly on the Holy Spirit or on biblical truth.

The major sign we are Christians is that we love other Christians (see 1 John 3:14). The one word that appears over and over again describing how members of the body of Christ should relate to each other is love. Great power, healing, growth, fellowship, and fulfillment may be found within the body of Christ by any group of believers who will relate to each other in love as they were designed to relate.

4

Only The Dead Feel No Pain

Many people are seeking peace. There's nothing wrong with that, but often people seem to assume that conflict is inherently bad or that the ideal life would be one that is conflict free. Anybody that is conflict free, I would suspect, is not experiencing growth. In fact, they are probably dead.

All of us have within a childlike desire to experience instant solution of our problems. This desire is intensified by the fact that God sometimes does act so that instant healing or change takes place. That is a fact of biblical history, and it still occurs in specific cases. However, God most often seems to work through a process.

Many Christians make the grave error of wanting to be "temple-jumpers." Satan tempted Christ to demand a miracle from God by jumping off the temple and "trusting God" to save Him from harm (Matt. 4:5-7). Many people, under the guise of being spiritual, tell others that they should stop medication or not go to the doctor, but just rely on the Lord. If they had enough faith, they are told, they would not have to do various things that might involve them with a helping professional of some kind.

My conviction is that it is legitimate to pray for healing and deliverance and that God may give it. But we cannot demand a miracle. If there is a medical or psychological process that will help bring healing, that process is from God. To demand something else can be a sign of immaturity and temple-jumping.

Christian patients have told me after a long struggle with some emotional problem that they realize they have become stronger, have learned more about God, and have become better equipped to lead a constructive Christian life. This growth is not *in spite* of their emotional problems, but *because* of the process they have gone through in finding relief.

This is the point in 2 Corinthians 1:3-5: as God comforts us and leads us through problems, we become better equipped to help others. "What a wonderful God we have—He is the Father of our Lord Jesus Christ, the source of every mercy, and the One who so wonderfully comforts and strengthens us in our hardships and trials. And why does He do this? So that when others are troubled, needing our sympathy and encouragement, we can pass on to them this same help and comfort God has given us. You can be sure that the more we undergo sufferings for Christ, the more He will shower us with His comfort and encouragement."

It seems to be a fact of human nature that learning and growth, development and change require a process, and most often the important changes in us take place within the framework of struggle. But God does promise to comfort us and direct us through this growth-producing conflict.

Saints in Process

We must understand who we are as Christians—not finished saints who have arrived at our ultimate destination of perfect likeness to Jesus Christ but "saints in process." And conflict is an integral part of that process.

A doctor from eastern Tennessee, somewhat disgruntled, once said, "Nobody will come to the doctor unless he is hurting or bleeding." Similarly, most of us will not change unless we are hurting in some way emotionally. Conflict motivates. C. S. Lewis, in a profound book called *The Problem of Pain*, states that God whispers to us in our joys and shouts to us in our pain. Very often, that is true; and we don't hear until He shouts.

Emotional pain, like physical pain, tells us that something is wrong and some changes need to be made. One of the more serious physical conditions a person can develop is to be insensitive to pain in some area of his body. Such a person will get something minor wrong, a thorn in his foot or a pebble in his shoe, and he doesn't even know it until he's got a big ulcer there. Or he leans on a "counter" and, unfortunately, he happens to be leaning on the hot top of a stove, and the first things he notices is the smell of burning flesh.

To survive, we need to be able to experience pain. Pain is a danger signal that lets us know something is wrong, and a change needs to take place.

That's the way it is with emotional pain.

One concept I sincerely try to impress on people who come to me with emotional problems is: *You have the possibility of ending up a stronger person not in spite of this trouble that you're going through, but because of it. You are going to learn some things about yourself and others that you otherwise might not face. Because you're hurting, you are motivated. You want to get out of this. And growth comes through conflict.*

The Psalmist said, "Before I was afflicted I went astray, but now have I kept Thy Word. It is good for me that I have been afflicted, that I might learn Thy statutes" (Psalm 119:67, 71, KJV). Many Christians have experienced similar benefit as they have learned and grown as a result of their afflictions.

I should say, growth comes *potentially* through conflict because, tragically, some people suffer for nothing. Whether we like it or not, pain puts us at a crossroads. We will either become bitter, critical, insulted, pessimistic, defeated, angry; or we will be forced into a path that will help us develop in our relationships with God and with people. Growth comes by facing conflicts and dealing with them.

One of the real hindrances to growth is that we often are not honest about conflict. We have this naive view: *Oh, a Christian shouldn't have that problem.* Or, *a Christian shouldn't have these difficulties.* And we won't honestly talk about it, deal with it, or work through it.

We should not be surprised when troubles come. In fact, we read in James 1:2-4, "Dear brothers, is your life full of difficulties and temptations? Then be happy, for when the way is rough, your patience has a chance to grow. So let it grow, and don't try to squirm out of your problems. For when your patience is finally in full bloom, then you will be ready for anything, strong in character, full and complete."

We should not try to hide the fact that we are having problems from our fellow Christians. This attitude denies the integrity of the body of Christ. Christians should talk over and pray over their problems. This is our right, our privilege, our responsibility.

The Idealized Self

Another concept we need to get straight in order to understand who we are as Christians relates to our identity, our self-concept. Of course, as Christians we know we are joint heirs with Christ, sons of God, those accepted and beloved of the Father. But there is another dimension to this matter of identity. It involves the idealized self; how you feel your behavior and character should actually be in everyday life.

This latter idealized self-image may be very complex. It is influenced not only by the discrepancy that exists between our image-of-God nature and our egocentric twist, but also by all sorts of "shoulds" and "oughts," some legitimate and some illegitimate, that have been imposed on us by parents or others from the past. It also includes our own self-imposed "shoulds" that are not necessarily valid for who God intends us to be.

The greater the gap between a person's idealized self and his actual or realized self, the greater dislike for himself or insecurity he will have. Growth has to do with dealing with this gap.

It is important to realize that the self-ideal can be quite distorted and involve all sorts of neurotic mechanisms. The distortions usually involve a person trying to base his identity on some transient quality. In order for him to be OK, he must be the strongest, prettiest, smartest, biggest, richest, sexiest, and so forth.

Such a person may have a driven quality to his

life. It seems he is trying to prove something to someone. Possibly a parent drilled into him that he is not a worthwhile person unless he is the best. Maybe he developed these drives to cover various feelings of insecurity. In any case, he is pursuing a false ego ideal. He may need to be loved by everyone in order for his world to seem right, and he is frequently frustrated.

Even the person who seems humble or self-depreciating may be going on a more subtle form of ego trip. Such people are often very fearful of being criticized, so they try to beat the world to the punch and criticize themselves. By implying that they should be so much better than they are, they are also actually saying, "I have such high ideals, really much higher than the average man." So the recognition that they are falling short still communicates an implied superiority.

One's whole idealized self may be based on fantasy. Many Christians seem to understand the concept of being saved by grace, but they have missed the concept of being sustained by grace. We all tend to fall into the trap of a sort of neo-legalism that involves its own ego trip.

We seem to think it's all up to us to work our way to some higher plane. Many churches foster this neurotic notion by seemingly basing a person's spirituality on how many church programs he's involved in. Each church group may develop its own list of neo-legalistic requirements to be a "super Christian."

To the degree that we are not firmly grounded in all that is implied in being saved by grace, we are vulnerable to letting other people impose upon us what they say we should be doing. These activities may or may not be what God intends for us.

The more we are vulnerable to accepting roles we can't fulfill, the greater the gap grows between our ideal and our performance, with ensuing frustration and guilt.

Nothing to Prove

But what *should* we do? We should rest in our identity in Jesus Christ, and say without being haughty, "Hey, I'm OK, I'm great. I love God. I'm marvelously created by Him, His crown of creation. God knew what He was doing when He put me together, and He loves me and has a plan for me. Furthermore, Christ loves me so much that He died for me to free me from the ego trip I tend to go on, and He indwells me. *I don't have to prove anything to anybody.*"

It's just great to have this kind of identity. When I get worried about how I'm going to overcome some problem and I don't see how I can do it, I suddenly discover there's a constant "I" in my concerns. I'm really saying it's all up to me, and I'm worried about what other people will think. Maybe "I" will not be considered the biggest or the best. It's as if I have no resource but myself. And this is an ego trip. When I come to grips with the fact that what I must do is turn it all over to God, and simply do my best knowing He loves me, knows all about me, created me, indwells me, and I don't have to prove to the world what a great person I am, I'm set free.

That doesn't mean I'm just going to lie down and curl up in a ball, which is the neurotic course to take. *Every truth can be given a slight twist that turns it into something destructive.* Certainly one of the destructive twists that you can give to what I have been saying is simply to think, "Well,

relationship. Some substitute doctrine for the personal, living relationship with Jesus Christ. If you believe a certain list of things about Him, you are OK. The ultimate sign of correctness, in this view, is simply to believe correctly.

This very easily becomes a defense mechanism against confronting oneself with the person of Jesus Christ, and against facing the question of how much of one's life is turned over to Him. One can hide behind his correct belief and display much littleness, bitterness, and meanness, still feeling all right because he believes correctly.

Of course, there are many churches that have very obscure doctrinal positions and that give little emphasis to the biblical facts about the person and work of Jesus Christ. Since these churches are not biblically oriented, we can view them with disapproval and really focus on how correctly we believe. Then we can very conveniently ignore the fact that we have substituted some statements about Jesus Christ for a growing relationship with Him that affects every area of life. If we do this, we will not experience the sense of identity, the growth, and the maturity we have discussed earlier.

Don'ts

There are people who substitute don'ts for Jesus Christ. They have a whole list of things that they do not do, and these are their badge, the sign of their Christianity. Like those who are "doctrine only" Christians, "don't" Christians are sometimes some of the meanest people I encounter. They apparently sleep very comfortably at night. They can ignore how cruel they may be with their children, their wives, or with other people, since they are very righteous because of all these things they don't do.

Deborah's father was such a man. Deborah was a college girl who came for help because she had an unreasonable fear of standing in front of a group of people. This was interfering with her plan to pursue a teaching career. Her father was an extremely religious, self-righteous man, who primarily focused on what a person should not do in order to be a Christian. One of the don'ts on his list was makeup for women. When a woman who used makeup joined his church, he left it and forced his family to do the same.

He also sexually molested his daughters.

The more a person substitutes don'ts for a living, ongoing relationship with Jesus Christ, the more likely he is to ignore glaring defects and anti-Christian attitudes or behavior in his life.

Doing

Many people substitute doing for Jesus Christ. They may be extremely active within a church organization and equally active in society. They may be doing worthwhile things, but to the degree that they are substituting doing for the personal relationship with Jesus Christ, they are not authentically Christian in their living. They are going on their own type ego trip, trying to save themselves. In fact, their very busyness may become a defense mechanism against honestly looking at themselves and recognizing the vacuum that exists.

John was a successful businessman in his 40s. He came from a wealthy family and was involved in managing a large enterprise. Virtually all his emotional energy was tied up in operating the business, and doing things which interested him.

John's wife felt neglected and angry. Yet, because John was a "good husband and provider," she felt guilty about her anger, and as a result became depressed.

John felt he was providing for his family very well, and that his wife was unreasonable and demanding.

John had an extreme need to be in the spotlight. This aspect of his egocentricity was reflected even in his alleged conversion experience. After John professed to become a Christian, he began to give rather dramatic testimonies around the country and to give of his time and money to various worthwhile causes.

However, the basic style of his life remained unchanged. He continued to neglect his family, abuse alcohol, and was involved with other women.

By his sheer busyness, John avoided facing his problems. He would not come in for counseling after the first visit, and claimed the problem was his wife's, not his.

Like John, some people who are very busy are actually trying to keep one step ahead of the spectre of emptiness and meaninglessness. They are just active enough to bring some sense of fulfillment, and they don't have to look at the real poverty of their relationship with the Lord, if indeed they have one.

Did

Some people substitute what they did for Jesus Christ—*the past*. "When I walked the aisle . . ."/ "When I became a Christian . . ."/"When I had this experience . . ." Their whole concept of Christianity is incorporated in some past experience which, they believe, brought them into the fold, and that's it. To the degree that this becomes a substitute for the ongoing personal relationship with Jesus Christ, who lovingly invades every aspect of one's existence, there will be something missing.

Development

Then there is the person who substitutes development for a personal relationship with Jesus Christ. Such a person might be called a cultural Christian. This refers to the person who has been reared in a Christian home and who essentially views Christianity as ethics, as responsibility, as respectability, as church-going—all of which are part of a culture. To the degree that one substitutes his development and his Christian cultural environment for a personal relationship with Jesus Christ, he will not experience new birth, new life, and new identity.

Dramatics

Others substitute dramatics for Christ. That is, they substitute dramatic experiences for the tough, obedient, ongoing personal relationship with Jesus Christ. For some, Christianity is all ecstatic experience. The discipline of Bible study, of obedience, of following our Lord in a responsible manner may be grossly minimized. One caught up in the dramatic focuses on experiences and feelings.

But feelings are very capricious, and the more dependent we are on how we happen to feel as a basis for evaluating our spiritual status, the more vulnerable we will be to peaks and valleys. This predisposes us to instability.

Let's summarize some of the vital points we need to understand clearly concerning our identity as Christians, as we have developed them in this and the preceding chapter.

1. We are the objects of Satan's attacks. Unless we recognize this, we place ourselves at a great disadvantage, even though we actually have superior resources at our command through our relationship to Christ.

2. We are sons of God and joint heirs with Jesus Christ. A conscious and continual reaffirming of this truth will help us meet all attacks of Satan with increasing strength and sense of adequacy.

3. Conflict is part of life. Instant solution to all our problems is not the Christian's birthright. God can often do far more for us through a process of growth or healing than He could by simply taking away all difficulties.

4. Our standing with God is perfect, but our state or actual personal condition is not. We must rest in the acceptance with God that we already have in Christ, but we must also keep growing toward personal conformity to the image of Christ.

5. We must resist any tendency to substitute other things, however good they may be in themselves, for a personal, living relationship with Jesus Christ in which every aspect of our thinking, feeling, and behavior is more and more centered around and influenced by Him.

As we resist the many subtle twists that can distort these principles, we will begin to find the abundant life that Jesus intends us to enjoy.

5

A Psychiatrist
Looks at
Christianity

Through the years Christians have been called everything from a cannibalistic Jewish sect to heavenly gourmets looking for pie in the sky. If you were to ask a hundred people at random to make a statement about the basic nature of Christianity, you would very likely conclude that the word Christian has lost its significance.

Here is a sample of phrases you would hear:

    Being good.

    Trying my best.

    Living by the golden rule.

    Going to church.

    Being baptized.

    Paying my bills.

    Being religious.

    Not being a heathen.

    Loving everybody.

    Not doing certain things (people usually pick things *they* do not happen to do for this type of negative definition).

There will also be some statements about believing the Bible or believing in Jesus, some given with great understanding and many without any understanding.

If you were to line up 100 mental health professionals and ask the same question, you would fare no better.

A large number of mental health professionals believe that Christianity encourages neurosis. Sigmund Freud stated it bluntly: "Religion is the universal obsessional neurosis of humanity."

Later in the same book he says, "Your religious doctrines will have to be discarded no matter whether the first attempts fail or whether the first substitute informations prove to be unstable" (*The Future of an Illusion,* Doubleday Anchor Books, New York, N.Y.).

In an earlier work, Freud wrote, "Religion is an attempt to get control over the sensory world in which we are placed by means of the wish world which we have developed inside us . . . It will not achieve its ends. Its doctrines bear . . . the stamp of the times in which they originated, the ignorant childlike days of the human race" (*New Introductory Lectures on Psychoanalysis,* W. W. Norton & Co., New York, N.Y.).

Freud and many other psychiatrists have charged Christianity with being particularly harmful in provoking guilt. In their view, Christianity imposes "outmoded" cultural norms from the past, prescribes standards of behavior no longer relevant, and thus simply increases a person's guilt. As they see it, people already feel too guilty, and don't need to have any more guilt heaped upon them.

As a further indictment, these psychiatrists claim that Christianity believes in myths and encourages magical thinking. A person entangled in this "wish world" must use mechanisms of denial and repression to defend against the real world. Neuroses are bound to follow.

A further criticism of Christianity is that it belittles man. Some people like to cite a line from the song "At the Cross" as an example: "Would He devote that sacred head for such a worm as I?" This description of man as a worm is seen as typical of Christianity's demeaning of man, who very often already has a poor self-image and hardly needs further belittlement.

There is, we must admit, a core of truth behind this thinking. Mental health professionals who hold this view of Christianity have accurately described ways in which people have often distorted and misapplied Christian truths. But this is the *only* significant truth to be found in this approach to Christianity.

Unfortunately, there *are* many Christians who live under an inappropriate burden of guilt. There are many Christians who have a style of provoking guilt in others in an unhealthy fashion. (But the neurotic twist or kink also may go in just the opposite direction. The Scriptures may be used to rationalize unchristian behavior, and to promote a sense of self-righteousness.)

Christians often do use the mechanisms of denial and repression. That is, they become less than honest and aware about their own feelings, problems, and behavior.

Not a Neurotic Mechanism

However, it is no more logical to conclude that Christianity is basically a neurotic process because it is often distorted than to conclude that physics is intrinsically evil because it was used to make the atom bomb. Of course, Christian truths can be twisted, kinked, or misapplied and bring suffering rather than help. This says something about the person twisting them and nothing about Christianity. Every truth from any source can be given a slight twist that changes it from truth to untruth, from being constructive to being destructive.

Actually, far from demeaning man, Christianity elevates man to the highest conceivable levels. It teaches that he is created only a little lower than the angels, that he has been given dominion over all the earth and made responsible for it, that the very hairs of his head are numbered, that the ineffable God loves him so much He has taken the incredible action of *becoming a man* Himself in order for man to have a personal relationship with Him.

So, it is Christianity that most elevates man. And, ironically, it is the humanist position that belittles man, for it denies him any ultimate or eternal destiny or meaning. Indeed, unbelief makes both man and the worm mere meaningless nothings, the blind, accidental result of time plus chance.

But while the Bible exalts man, it also is honest about man's imperfections. It points out that, though man is created in the image of God, it is his universal experience to go his own way, to call the shots himself, to rebel against the authority of God, and, basically, to make an idol of himself. This separates him from God and prevents him from functioning as God designed him to function. This is simply the truth about man. This is where we are, and this is why we need saving.

Not Just Faith in Faith

Today there are increasing numbers of professionals who have decided that Christianity or some kind of "faith" might not be so bad after all. If you believe in something outside yourself, if you have strong faith in it, you are less likely to be overwhelmed by uncertainty, conflicts, and, ultimately, death.

A person of faith may be less self-centered, have a greater sense of responsibility, adhere more faithfully to ethical standards, and exhibit more stability in his life than he would without faith.

Erich Fromm, in his book, *Art of Loving* (Colophon Books, Harper and Row, N.Y., N.Y., 1956), suggests that if a man has a mature concept of God, it can be constructive. But he says, "Quite obviously the majority of people have in their personal development not overcome this infantile stage, and hence the belief in God to most people is the belief of a helping father—a childish illusion."

Fromm, a prolific writer on psychological themes, indicates that he has faith in the principles which "God" represents. In other words, he, like Freud, believes that God is only an idea invented by people to meet their various needs, but, unlike Freud, he thinks that the idea of God does have some useful possibilities.

C. G. Jung, the founder of analytic psychology, had an even more positive view of religion. He wrote, "Among all my patients over 35, there has not been one whose problem, in the last resort, was not that of finding a religious outlook on life. They fell ill when they had lost that which the living religions of every age have given. None has been healed who did not regain his religious outlook" (*Modern Man in Search of a Soul,* Harcourt Brace Jovanovich, N.Y., N.Y.).

Jung, however, like other psychiatrists who simply view faith in general as helpful to mental health, did not profess belief in an infinite personal God, but only believed that a religious view of life gives meaning and significance.

In this view, the object of faith is largely irrelevant. The object of such faith may be a totem pole in the backyard. It may be some vague existential concept of God. Or such faith may be a mystical belief in forces or spirits that indwell everybody and everything.

The possibility of there being an infinite and personal and knowable God who literally and specifically can change one's life, over and above the psychology of having faith in faith, is generally ignored or denied by people who hold this view. This faith in faith is probably the majority view in the mental health field today.

There is, no doubt, an element of truth behind this thinking by mental health professionals. Commitment to something outside oneself obviously can have positive psychological effects. But if what a person believes is not ultimately true, he must distort reality. And the more his beliefs are not verified by his experience, the more distortion of reality or the more mental conflict he will experience. We need the certainty the Apostle Paul expressed when he said, "I *know* whom I have believed" (2 Tim. 1:12, KJV).

The real question is whether there actually *is* Someone there who acts in history and deals with us over and above just how we happen to feel or believe. If we're going to base our life on faith, we'd be much better off with faith in reality than with faith in a delusion.

This is especially true when we consider ultimate results. The Bible says it is appointed unto man once to die and after that the judgment (see

·Heb. 9:27). A false and delusive substitute for faith in God will finally leave man standing naked and empty before God.

Not Just Being Loving

There are many counselors who identify themselves as religious or Christian who seem to believe that Christianity consists solely of developing honesty, openness, and love in human relationships. Such people may talk little about the propositional truths of Scripture. They may be impatient with or seemingly indifferent toward sound doctrine. Relationships and attitudes are everything.

We are told to behave in a loving, open, honest, warm fashion toward each other. Often, however, those who take this view do not concern themselves with *how* a person is to be able to relate this way. They tend to overlook the basic internal problem (misposition before God, egocentricity) that blocks a person from being able to do this at a deeper level in the first place.

This approach fails to come to grips either with man's basic nature or the essential nature of Christianity. Man needs radical internal change in order to acquire greater capacities and motivations to love, and Christ can give these capacities. Furthermore, Christianity is not just an adjunct to good mental health. True Christianity is Christ-centered and man-related. Those we have been describing reverse that, making their message man-centered and Christ-related.

It is true, of course, that love is the central aspect of Christianity. We are told that God is love, and that we are to love Him and our neighbor. The Apostle John says that one of the signs of salvation is love: "If we love other Christians it proves that we have been delivered from hell and given eternal life. But a person who doesn't have love for others is headed for eternal death" (1 John 3:14).

The claim of Christianity is that however loving a person may be naturally, he can become more loving. Some people naturally find it very difficult to be loving. Others are outgoing and loving from the very beginning. But whatever one's natural capacities are, under the Lordship of Christ they are enhanced and enriched through a growing process.

Not a Happily-Ever-After Life

Another view, held by extremely few in the mental health field but held in one form or another by a huge number of Christians, is that if a person will simply get right with God—become a Christian, become saved, walk the aisle, get sprinkled, dunked, hosed, rivered, baptized, or whatever—his problems will be over. He now has it made in the kingdom of God, and he should not have any emotional problems. If you do have emotional problems and claim to be a Christian, there will be doubt whether you really are a Christian, or whether you are a *good* Christian.

This is one of the more destructive views of Christianity that I know about. Many Christians smile knowingly in seeming agreement when I say this. But when the chips are down and these very people are in my office with emotional problems, they suffer from the same misconception. Their attitude is: I really should not be having these problems. If I were a good enough Christian, if I would just pray a little harder, the problems should go away.

When will we really face the fact that becoming

a Christian does not guarantee a person freedom from emotional problems or mental anguish? Jesus said, "Here on earth you will have many trials and sorrows; but cheer up, for I have overcome the world" (John 16:33). Christians are not automatically filled with joy and peace in one continuing experience. When a Christian does have emotional problems, they may not go away with prayer. That does not mean he is not "really" Christian. It does not necessarily mean he only needs to pray harder or have some additional, possibly ecstatic, experience.

People who hold this "happily-ever-after" view are subject to increasing doubt. If the promises they heard about Christianity solving all problems are not proven true (at least not on their terms nor by their time schedule), possibly none of it is true.

Another reaction is to become angry at God for not living up to His promises. These reactions add guilt, doubt, and anger to the suffering already present.

The view that if one would just become a Christian, all his problems would be over, also has a powerful core of truth to it. After all, this is the central need we all do have. Clearly there are many people who feel guilty because they are guilty. They don't need a set of slick psychological rationalizations to explain why they do what they do. They need to cut it out and get right with the Lord and begin to function as God designed them.

Not a Poor, Second-Best Psychology

Many pastors and many lay people have been seduced or intimidated by the mystique of psychology. They regard the mental health profession with the sort of awe once felt for witch doctors or mystics. And the Bible is relegated to an inferior position.

O. Hobart Mowrer says, "Has evangelical religion sold its birthright for a mess of psychological pottage? In attempting to rectify their disastrous early neglect of psychopathology, have the churches and seminaries assimilated a viewpoint and value system more destructive and deadly than the evil they were attempting to eliminate? As a psychologist and churchman, I believe the answer to these questions is in the affirmative." (*The Crisis in Psychiatry and Religion,* an Insight Book, Van Nostrand Reinhold, New York, N.Y.)

That is, Christians have sometimes concluded that the "real answers" to man's practical problems are outside the Bible somewhere. So they soft-pedal the Bible, and then they apply to "science" or "psychology" for the real answers. The result is a thinly disguised and often rankly amateurish psychology which poses as advanced Christianity.

I believe that Christianity is much more than a second-best source for the truth that heals, guides, corrects, and liberates. Actually the ongoing, growing Christian experience affords the most solid basis for a person to build a constructive, secure identity and to find fulfillment and meaning in his life. And the Bible is without question the most profound and at the same time the most practical and valid resource book for psychological insight ever written. It tells us who we are, and how we are to relate to God and each other. It reveals God's truth and how the universe works. People who order their lives as if the Bible were not true or relevant to them are in fact fighting against reality.

What Christianity Is

I have said Christianity is not a neurotic mechanism. It is, then, a realistic, healing, elevating system of truth.

I have said Christianity is not just faith in faith. It is, then, a faith in one living and true God as He is made known to us by the Holy Spirit in and through Jesus Christ.

I have said Christianity is not just being loving. It is, then, propositional truth which leads us into loving and constructive relationships, and also reveals the true nature of God and all His works.

I have said Christianity is not a happily-ever-after life. It is, then, a continuing struggle, but one in which we can triumph through the power of Christ, and one in which even our defeats, as well as our victories, can contribute to our spiritual and personal growth.

I have said that Christianity is not a poor, second-best psychology. It is, then, the well-spring of relational truth, the best possible source and supply of a well-integrated life.

How I Became a Christian

Admittedly, I have written this chapter not only as a psychiatrist looking at Christianity but as a Christian looking at psychiatry. You have a right to know the background from which I write, how and why I became a Christian.

I grew up going to Sunday School and church. When I was 12, I joined a church. In my case, this didn't include any kind of awareness of sin or of salvation or of the reality of Jesus Christ. It was the year I joined the Boy Scouts, and it seemed logical to join the church too.

I became a church member and remained a

church member. I absorbed the doctrines of the church and agreed with them, but they had little effect on my life.

When I began my studies at Princeton University and took some religion courses along with my pre-med, it was obvious that my professors didn't believe the Scriptures were fully trustworthy. I read many books that suggested the same concept. All of this had a curious effect on me. These people were working so hard to try to disprove the Scripture that I began to see they did not have a strong case. So it only strengthened my faith.

But my "faith" was more an intellectual awareness than it was a matter of having the Lord indwell me.

In medical school I was so busy I hardly gave Christ any thought. I married Betsy while I was in medical school and afterward went into the Air Force. Then Betsy's mother, who was an alcoholic, moved to Orlando, Fla., where I was stationed. She was a brilliant woman—a court reporter—and could get a job anywhere, anytime. But because of her alcohol problem, we got into one crisis after another with her. Finally we asked Pastor Jim Haskins at a little neighborhood church for help.

He came and talked to us, and, in passing, he asked, "Well, are you all Christians?"

"Of course," we said. I had been a church member for 18 years. What else would I be?

But Betsy and I realized something was missing in our lives and we admitted it. The pastor said, "OK, if you want to experience some growth, start reading the Bible regularly, praying, coming to church regularly, seeing what it's all about. Just become involved."

So almost like in organic chemistry lab when I

was obediently following the manual without much understanding of what I was doing and hoping it wouldn't blow up, I decided to try this as an experiment. It was as simplistic as that. I started reading the Scriptures and going to church regularly. We also started tithing our income.

In the average church when someone gets active, the leaders start asking him to do things. "Teach this class," they said, so I started teaching a class. The next thing I knew they had appointed me the chairman of the annual revival, a series of evangelistic meetings. I had a very good friend, who, by his own admission, was not a Christian but was seeking. I hoped the revival would be a means of reaching him. I decided to arm myself with the Scriptures to help my friend.

I discussed the verses that point out we all need a Saviour, that, as a matter of fact, we all strike out on the very first commandment: to "love the Lord thy God with all thy heart, soul, strength. and mind and thy neighbor as thyself." I cited the Scriptures that make clear that all have sinned and come short of the glory of God. I also used the Scriptures that point out how Jesus is Lord and Saviour, the significance of the Atonement and the Resurrection, the importance of faith, and of putting faith into action.

My friend listened appreciatively to what I had to say, but to my knowledge, he never made a commitment. However, a few days later, it suddenly hit me like a brick that all these truths that I had known intellectually and had gotten together to share with my friend were really not mine. I had really never faced the fact of *my sin*, my basic self-centeredness, my subtle rebellion against God. I had been able to see Christ as Saviour in an intellectual way, but I had never repented nor committed my life to Him.

Betsy had been going through a similar process of moving from an intellectual belief to a personal commitment. The upshot of it all was that the chairman of the revival and his wife walked the aisle when the invitation was given to openly receive and confess Christ.

How I Became a Psychiatrist

The most immediate thing Christ did for me after my conversion was to give me a new identity. I was driving down Colonial Boulevard in Orlando shortly after my conversion, thinking about what had happened in my life, and it suddenly hit me that I *had eternal life now*. It was not something off in the future. I remember smiling, as I drove along, at the realization that I am a joint heir with Christ, a child of God, that I am part of God's family, that God has plans for me, and as I make myself available to Him, really exciting things are in store for me.

This new identity was very meaningful for me, because as a youngster I was always trying to compensate for being scrawny and red headed. And now I was a son of God!

Our marriage took on new meaning and our relationship began to improve as Betsy and I both became less self-centered. My way of viewing the world also changed. Life began to make sense. Some of our practices changed. There were places we had gone or things we had done that just didn't fit into our lives any more, so they dropped away without our getting into some kind of self-righteous kick. I also had a new sense that I was fitting in with the will and purposes of God. It was as if I had begun going with the flow of the universe instead of against it.

My conversion also had a big effect on my concept of medical practice. I was chief of the out-patient clinic at the air base, where we saw a tremendous number of patients. Now, I began to see them as *people* with spiritual as well as physical needs. I began to realize that a huge percentage of those who came to this very out-patient clinic had psychological and spiritual problems. As a result, I decided to go into psychiatry, though when I left medical school, I thought psychiatry was the last thing I would ever consider.

What really impelled me into psychiatry, then, was recognizing the tremendous relationship between Christianity and mental health. I felt that if only we could bring spiritual and psychological truths together, we could really help people, instead of putting Band-Aids on mortal wounds, so to speak. So, I went into my residency at Duke University with the express purpose of becoming a psychiatrist and putting Christianity and mental health together if I could.

I already knew that basic psychiatric theories about man's nature and his needs for mental health were not based on the Bible and in some instances were antibiblical. However, I learned in my three years of residency that secular psychiatry has an immense amount of truth to teach. I learned that there are many complex medical aspects of emotional problems. There are many valid techniques to help people open up better. And there are many different mechanisms and motivations which influence people.

My psychiatry residency really was no threat to my Christianity. I already had heard, at one time or another, the various arguments or rationalizations against Christianity, and for me Christianity made the most sense. Belief that there is no personal God can only be maintained by a "faith" of a kind, which assumes some sort of blind forces brought everything into being.

One must have a base of authority, ultimately, on which he decides what to believe and what to reject. My base was Scripture, and I believe it reveals the true nature of man and his needs.

I also observed that, in many points, unbelieving "authorities" do not agree among themselves. So I sought to ferret out the truth and the untruth in that which was presented to me.

When I was a first-year resident, my supervisor had little use for Christianity. Once I was describing my treatment program of an alcoholic patient to him, and I referred to the spiritual need this man had. My point was that when he left alcoholism, he was going to have a vacuum in his life. He would need to fill that vacuum with God. My supervisor thought that was sort of far-out and made a joke about it.

Six years later, I saw this same doctor at a gathering of psychiatrists. He gave me a great big grin and raised his hand to me from across the room. When we got together, he related his dramatic conversion to Christ. Today he is speaking all over the country on the importance of Christianity to every aspect of life.

Only Jesus Christ is ultimately able to say, "I am the way, the truth, and the life; no man cometh unto the Father but by Me" (John 14:6, KJV).

Part III

What Are Our Needs?

6

A Many Splendored Or Much Splintered Thing

A European schoolmaster was teaching his class religious knowledge some years ago. "Why did Jesus come into the world?" he asked, reviewing what the students were already supposed to know.

There was no answer.

"Why did Jesus come?" he shouted, exasperated.

Still no answer.

"*Love!*" he roared, marching around the room and hitting each child on the head with his ruler. "Love! Love! Love!"

And so He did.

But somehow that love has not taken hold of the whole human race. And even those who have their "religious knowledge" down pat often have their love relationships severely distorted, kinked.

Love is the most powerful healing force that can exist in an individual's life. People who are sure they are loved have a tremendous amount going for them to counter any kind of destructive forces, neuroses, or serious conflicts. Perfect love really does cast out fear. But there are many tremendous distortions and incorrect ideas about love. Tragically, much twisted love comes from Christians themselves.

Some of the bitterest attacks on Christians come from other Christians. Some groups in their inestimable egocentricity and pride think they are the only ones left in the world who are true to the Word. They say, as Elijah did in his depression, "I even I only am left" (1 Kings 19:10, KJV). Their primary approach to people is to judge them. Jesus said, "I demand that you love each other, for you get enough hate from the world!" (John 15:17, 18)

Paul wrote to the Philippians, "Is there any such thing as Christians cheering each other up? Do you love me enough to want to help me? Does it mean anything to you that we are brothers in the Lord, sharing the same Spirit? Are your hearts tender and sympathetic at all? Then make me truly happy by loving each other and agreeing wholeheartedly with each other, working together with one heart and mind and purpose.

"Don't be selfish; don't live to make a good impression on others. Be humble, thinking of others as better than yourself" (Phil. 2:1-3).

How prone we are to go on our own "Christian" ego trips and attack each other because "only we are true to the Word; only we have not bowed to Baal." Such guardians of Christianity (as they see it) have often substituted don'ts and doctrine for the personal relationship with Jesus Christ that allows Him to act in one's life more and more so that one is able to love better and better.

The Centrality of Love
Love is absolutely central in Scripture. God is described as love. All the law is fulfilled in love to the

Lord and to man. John flatly states that if you aren't loving you aren't a Christian (see 1 John 4:8). In each of his letters, Paul admonished Christians to act in love. Peter writes of growth beyond initial faith in terms of adding to faith the qualities of virtue, knowledge, self-control, patience, godliness, brotherly affection, and love (see 2 Peter 1:5-9). Apparently many Christians are still stuck at stage one; they have faith, but rather than experiencing Christian growth, they spend most of their emotional energy in suspecting others of having inadequate faith, or they just don't relate faith with life.

Love is more than correct belief and doctrine. However, at the other end of the pendulum's swing are those who focus heavily on loving but have inadequate faith to back it up or to live it as Christ intended. There is much talk today about love. "What the world needs now is love, sweet love." We're told we should build a new system of ethics with love as the ultimate guideline to reality. But the crucial issue is not faced in many of the ethical systems based on love. I refer to the problem that Jeremiah described so well, "The heart is deceitful above all things and desperately wicked" (Jer. 17: 9, KJV).

Without a Scriptural base on which to build, phrases about love become meaningless and empty. That is, unless there is a new birth, a life-changing faith on which to build, "love" can very quickly become doing what you feel like doing, covered up by all sorts of rationalizations. "Love" may be readily converted to manipulation so that it is nothing less than the old sinful ego trip in new clothing.

For love to be as God intended and as man needs, we must experience a revolutionary change from being egocentric to becoming Christocentric. And then we must begin the often painful process of honestly revealing ourselves to God so that every aspect of what we say and do is open to Him. This is, in part, what John meant by "walking in the light" (see 1 John 1:7). Only when we bring ourselves humbly and openly into the light—the truth of Scripture—can we experience fellowship, cleansing, and fulfillment. Love is more than trying to behave magnanimously on your own terms, within your own strength and knowledge.

More Than Feelings

Love is often further distorted by a romantic or mystical concept that pervades our culture. Here the focus is almost exclusively on feelings. This twisted view has been given even stronger impetus in our present society by a dominant philosophy that says there are no absolute truths. Therefore, each man must do his own thing. If it feels good, do it. French philosopher René Descartes' famous statement, "I think; therefore I am," now becomes, "I feel; therefore I am—I hope."

I see many couples who are experiencing and giving much pain because they have tried to base their lives on such a "by feelings" philosophy. Premarital sexual relations increase the chances that a relationship will develop along these lines because premarital sex focuses so strongly on feelings without responsibility and commitment. A couple may come together because the chemistry was right, or the Zodiac sign was right, or it just felt like the right thing to do. But when it comes down to the real nitty-gritty of living together, of making a bridge-burning commitment to each other, their "love" falls apart. So they look for a new partner, searching for the golden fleece, for the situation in which their feelings will always be just right. And, of course, history will soon repeat, because love is more than feelings.

More Than Sacrifice

Some see love as sacrifice. In this setting, the more a person does for someone else, the more he loves. Of course, there is a powerful core of truth here, but sometimes service rendered becomes a substitute for the personal relationship that must accompany love at its best.

Usually to the bewilderment of the person loving this way, those on the receiving end often seem ungrateful or even resentful. Love that gives service but does not give the person in a sharing, open, give-and-take relationship causes the recipient to feel weak, dependent, and somehow beneath the giver.

Mothers who have "sacrificed all for their children" often find just such a situation. They may not only have hostile, rebellious children but also a hostile husband. The cycle often begins with a husband believing that loving his wife means paying the bills, getting ahead, buying education, conveniences, trips, and gadgets. Apart from financing the family, he is not personally involved very much.

Mother needs above all to share in a life and feel she has something unique to contribute. Since husband closes the door—"What do you mean I don't care? I buy you everything you want"—she turns to the children and becomes over-involved with them. She knocks herself out for them, and they become more demanding and less appreciative.

She has left out a powerful ingredient of love:

giving a person what he needs, not necessarily what he wants. And the consistent discipline the children desperately need is usually absent in this setting, particularly since the father has long since abdicated his role in this area.

Love is more than doing for someone.

Blocks to Love

Love is a universal need, and yet we seem to have great difficulty in giving and receiving love in a consistent manner. Many songs give us insights into the blocks to loving. Freud said dreams are the royal road to the unconscious. In many ways, the songs we sing and with which we identify serve the same purpose. They reveal much about our hopes, fears, doubts, feelings. For example, the song "Bridge Over Troubled Water" by Paul Simon was tremendously popular. It captures and expresses the tremendous need we all have to give and receive love. It describes a commitment to love when others have deserted, when there is darkness and pain. It expresses a consistency in loving. It does not tell how to arrive at this state, but it certainly expresses what we all desire.

"I Am a Rock" by the same author reveals one of the basic problems in loving, which is ultimately fear—fear of being hurt, rejected, abused, used. The song describes a person who builds strong walls, who virtually secludes himself in a great fortress that no one can penetrate. He insists he does not need friendship. Nor does he want it, because it causes pain. He knows this from bitter experience, and even the memory is painful to him. He reasons that if he had not loved he would not have been hurt. So now he has become an island, a rock, so that he will not hurt or cry ever again.

One response to discovering by hard experience that one cannot give and receive love in its deepest dimensions is withdrawal. This is a natural reaction whenever we are hurt. It is risky to attempt loving because we may be hurt more. So we build walls to protect us from further hurt. All of us are wall-builders to some degree. And we can thus protect ourselves from some of the hurt that would come from reaching out and being rejected. But the walls also doom us to relatively superficial relationships, and they impoverish our lives. For in a very real sense, not to love is not to live.

Sometimes the first step toward learning truth in any area is to learn that we do not know the answers. This may also be the hardest step we must take. But no one is so hopelessly ignorant as he who does not know and who does not know that he does not know. While popular songs talk much of love, they do not all necessarily reflect any truth about love. The song "Both Sides Now" admits this confusion. It describes love first as a romantic feeling, and then, when this fails, the person becomes a wall-builder and manipulator, finally ending in confusion, not knowing what love is at all. When we try to base love on feelings only, or when we withdraw and simply use people, we can never really know love.

The distortions of love are too many to consider in detail here. Songs of both long ago and of the present express them. "Frankie and Johnnie were lovers," but she ends up shooting him. (He was her man, but he did her wrong by going out with someone else.)

If you "love" enough to let a guy stash his sleeping bag behind your couch whenever he wants to —without making any demands on him—you will always be gentle on his mind.

Then, there is the "love" that seems sweeter because it's forbidden. One woman has your love but the other has your name, and it's a shame how you have to sneak around, but hopefully your villainous partner will eventually release you and let you love again.

There are hundreds of songs about reactions to distorted love, from homicide to suicide to agonizing grief. But all reveal the powerful need and equally powerful and sometimes violent reactions to the need not being met.

Needed: A Radical Change

The most basic source of these blocks to giving and receiving love is egocentricity. The blocks are expressions of the self-centeredness or the little infant that is inside all of us.

An infant, so far as he is concerned, is the center of the universe. Everything in this world exists for his welfare. Everything is either good or bad depending on how well it meets his needs. If it feels good, smells good, tastes good, it's good; and if it doesn't, it's bad. The infant really, functionally, has usurped the position of God as the sole evaluator and the center of the universe. And we all carry this attitude within us.

Probably from a biological standpoint, this attitude is important to the survival of the infant. You *know* when he needs some care! But this attitude persists in our adult lives. How quickly we go on ego trips, and act and react in ways designed to protect ourselves, to elevate ourselves, and to second guess what others may think about us. This is tremendously disruptive to our relationships with other people, with God, and even within ourselves.

This egocentricity problem is so engrained that none of the solutions the world offers will remove it. As needed and helpful as good environment and good education are, they do not eradicate this quality. A person may then simply be egocentric in a more sophisticated way. Certainly a constructive environment and education are helpful in presenting proper values and ethics to people. But they simply do not take away the internal, powerful egocentricity. In fact, some of the most destructive and bitter interactions among people are seen in those given every advantage of environment and education.

What is needed is a dramatic change, an internal shift, as described in the prophecies of Jeremiah and Ezekiel. They predicted that the time would come when the Lord would take out from man his heart of stone and put in its place a heart of flesh, would take out the cold, inanimate, unfeeling, dead heart, and replace it with something alive and responsive (see Jer. 24:7, 31:31-34; Ezek. 11:19, 20).

It is this principle exactly that Jesus had in mind when the well-educated, very religious Nicodemus came to Him and wanted to know really what it's all about. Jesus said, in effect, "Look, Nicodemus, you have to be born again. All of your religious piety simply will not lead you into the kingdom of God. A powerful internal change is necessary."

This is what Paul meant when he told the Corinthians, "If any man be in Christ, he is a new creature; old things are passed away; behold, all things are become new" (2 Cor. 5:17, KJV).

With Christ, a person has a new option that he did not have before. He has recognized his egocentricity, has finally been willing to face the fact of his tendency to rebel against God, has confessed

this and has committed himself to Christ. Such a
person has possibilities for being able to give
and receive love that he did not have before.

Defining Love

The most solid basis for the definition of love is
found in 1 John 4:10 (KJV): "Herein is love, not
that we loved God, but that He loved us and sent
His Son to be the propitiation for our sins." Any
definition of love that does not start here will be a
defective view of love, because it must rely on
man's alleged natural capacity to give and receive
love. And it will likely end up in either romanticism
or manipulation.

Christ's self-sacrifice is the ultimate expression
of the love of God. Through His death and resurrection, and our commitment to Him, we can experience in new ways the love of God, as well as
express it.

"He loved us and sent His Son" describes the
basic source and act of love. This love can operate
in us as we *shift from a self-centered to a Christ-
centered position.* We are now better able to follow
the divine commandment to put love into practice.
We have new capacities and new motivations to
love. The Apostle John gets hard-nosed about this.
He says we are liars if we claim to be Christians
but don't practice loving (see 1 John 4:20).

A person who has truly experienced this powerful love of God and who realizes how much he is
loved of God is also better able to love himself.
As many have recognized, without a healthy love
for ourselves, we are unable to love others. As we
properly love ourselves, we are less bound by self-
consciousness and do not need to spend so much
emotional energy trying to repair our sense of

worth. We are able to see others as persons rather than as objects we may use to patch up our egos.

One may think that loving self is the same thing as being egocentric, but the two are really worlds apart. Egocentricity centers everything around self; the self actually feels defective and weak, and has to extract from the world all it can to feel better. The kind of love for self that the new birth can bring frees the person from the egocentric position, because this type love gives to others rather than extracting from them.

Some may quickly object to this line of reasoning because they know people with no Christian commitment who are much more loving than someone else with a strong Christian commitment. However, love exists in the world at all only because we are created in the image of God, and even though we are fallen creatures, we still bear the imprint of that original design.

Thus all people have some capacity to love by virtue of their creation in God's image. Some have a greater capacity because of a happy arrangement of genes and chromosomes or because they were reared in a loving environment. Therefore some people are naturally much more loving, trusting, outgoing than others. But regardless of a person's "givens," if and when he turns himself over to Jesus Christ, he gains new capacities, new motivations, and clearer guidelines for living a life of love.

Some people who have become Christians are not naturally outgoing or loving and find it very difficult to love. At a given point in time, they may indeed be less loving than some nonbeliever. However, they are more loving than they would be if they were not Christians. A process to make them more loving has begun and will continue until those individuals are with the Lord.

Volitional Love

The tendency to think of love as some strong feeling which compels one to behave in a certain way is very common. Such confusion about the role of feelings in one's life often produces one of the points of resistance that we encounter in counseling. A person comes to a counselor with some kind of pain or problem and often has the idea that something mysterious is going to take place in the counseling session that will make his or her feelings change. After while he or she may be getting the message: you need to change a certain pattern, a certain behavioral response—whether you *feel* like it or not.

Then the resistance comes.

"My mother never loved me."

"I'm just that way."

"Everybody on my father's side of the family is like that."

"Ever since I had my operation, I've been this way."

"I can't."

"It would be hypocritical of me to change if I don't feel like it."

It seems to be so much easier to behave a certain way if one has a compelling feeling. Of course, any animal behaves on that frequency. There is nothing distinctively human and certainly nothing Christian about responding to a strong feeling, a motivation.

A crucial aspect of love is its volitional element. Love involves an act of the will, a choice, a commitment. The true characteristics of love are set forth in what is generally acknowledged to be one of the greatest passages of prose in the English language, 1 Corinthians 13. The Living Bible renders verses 1-7 as follows:

"If I had the gift of being able to speak in other languages without learning them, and could speak in every language there is in all of heaven and earth, but didn't love others, I would only be making noise. If I had the gift of prophecy and knew all about what was going to happen in the future, knew everything about *everything*, but didn't love others, what good would it do? Even if I had the gift of faith so that I could speak to a mountain and make it move, I would still be worth nothing at all without love. If I gave everything I have to poor people, and if I were burned alive for preaching the Gospel, but didn't love others, it would be of no value whatever.

"Love is very patient and kind, never jealous or envious, never boastful or proud, never haughty or selfish or rude. Love does not demand its own way. It is not irritable or touchy. It does not hold grudges and will hardly even notice when others do it wrong. It is never glad about injustice, but rejoices whenever truth wins out. If you love someone, you will be loyal to him no matter what the cost. You will always believe in him, always expect the best of him, and always stand your ground in defending him."

Notice that this beautiful passage describing love says nothing about feelings or emotions. Every single quality attributed to love is an attitude that we may have toward someone with an act of our will that is turned over to God.

It should be noted, however, that often powerful feelings will follow when a person makes such a commitment.

Is it hypocritical to say that you are angry with

someone or at the present time do not like someone but you still love that person? No, because regardless of your feelings, you can still be kind, patient, truthful, and resist being rude, selfish, jealous, or spiteful.

Particularly, love is not a score keeper or an injustice collector. Some of the most unhappy people that I see are those who are frequently getting their feelings hurt—avid injustice collectors, who habitually violate 1 Corinthians 13. Such people maintain a veritable museum in their minds: all of their injustice trophies are enshrined in glass, and they take strolls through the corridors of this museum, relishing trophies of all the injustices that have been committed against them. They take time to polish each one, all the time feeling hurt, martyred, and self-righteous over the fact that this wrong has been done to them. Love that heals does not keep score.

How to Have This Love

The kind of love 1 Corinthians 13 describes does not come naturally. In fact, it is a love that is consistently expressed only by God Himself. Only by having His Spirit indwelling us, coupled with our active commitment to obey, can this type of love grow and be expressed in us.

The world is dying for the lack of love. Why? Because we fail to exhibit obedience to Jesus Christ, with an act of the will displaying this love, this attitude toward others.

Pastor Jones had been in the ministry—and married—for about 15 years. When I first talked with him, he was very discouraged, was considering leaving the ministry, and was even wondering whether he could continue to live with his wife.

Mrs. Jones was very cold to him physically, and she was also very critical of his sermons and of him in general.

After he had described many of these frustrations, Pastor Jones was able to recognize that he refrained from doing many little things for his wife that she would have liked, whether it was being affectionate, or communicative, or doing some little chore around the house.

He became aware that he carried a general sense of resentment toward her, and that he had the attitude that he wasn't going to do these nice things for her because of the way she treated him.

He was challenged to put 1 Corinthians 13 into practice, which doesn't have any small print attached to the policy. He recognized he should love his wife unconditionally, without giving up on her, and without expecting something in return.

He was able to do this and was amazed at the changes that took place in only one or two weeks. His sermons were getting better, or at least his wife wasn't as critical. She was much more physically affectionate with him, and the entire escalating negative reaction to each other was reversed.

Several months later, I saw Pastor Jones again. He was still operating on this new principle of unconditional loving, and it had been very healing for them.

This is not to say that love is simply and only an attitude which anyone may choose to have. It is hardly that simple, and it may be far from easy. It took a lot of grace for Pastor Jones to go contrary to his natural inclinations and begin to show unconditional love toward his wife. But Pastor Jones had the grace it took. Or, more precisely, he appropriated grace from God to do the thing he knew he should do. Then, both his and his wife's feelings changed, and healing took place in their relationship.

The Bible teaches that love is the fruit of the Spirit (see Gal. 5:22, 23). As we make a commitment to obey Him, and as we trust Him for the grace that takes, He gives us the fullness of His Spirit, and love.

Love or its counterfeits, attempted on any basis other than this, will never bring the maximal fulfillment and healing that we need and may in fact be manipulative and destructive. God will give you the real thing, without which you are "worth nothing at all" (1 Cor. 13:3).

7

Do Not Fold,
Spindle,
or Mutilate

Shortly after moving to Atlanta, I discovered that one of my credit cards had gotten all fouled up. The company failed to recognize the change of address I had turned in and kept sending bills to my old address for charges I had already paid. Each time I would write, a computer responded with a routine print-out statement. I felt I was being ignored, that I was being reduced to a non-person. Finally I wrote a letter to the company, with a statement on the envelope, "Please let a human handle this." It got results.

We all feel the need to be treated as persons, to be considered of great worth and not just as numbers. I have dealt with many patients who had this need.

Bob was a very insecure man who always seemed to feel he had to prove himself to everybody. He tried to prove what a big man he was by gambling, by flirting with women, by working hard, by making deals, and by making a lot of money.

No matter what his successes were, he always had a need to present himself as being more successful than he actually was. This introduced a powerful drive to his life, as if he were only one step ahead of the reality that he was in many respects a phony.

His wheeler-dealer style of living caused his wife to mistrust him. She apparently had good reason; he had been unfaithful and untruthful to her at various times.

Bob's wife stayed upset because she was not first in his life. She reacted to his irresponsibility by often checking up on him, by saying little things to put him down, and by attempting to make him feel guilty. This was her way of expressing her anger and her fear that he was not being true to her.

Bob highly resented her accusations, her double-checking, and her statements that put him down. These things only aggravated his feelings of insecurity and inadequacy, and he defended against such feelings with even more wheeling and dealing, trying to look big. The couple went round and round in this fashion.

In counseling, Bob was able to recognize and express his tremendous fear of failure in every area of his life.

Part of Bob's fear was that he would appear weak or inadequate in the eyes of his wife. However, as he became more honest and revealed some of his fears, the wife's response was actually to admire him more, to trust him more, and to feel she was beginning to deal with a real person. This was sometimes a painful process for both Bob and his wife, as they faced reality, but only by doing so could healing take place in their relationship.

It is not coincidental that when Bob became more honest with himself and quit running, he could see his spiritual needs. As he began to turn his life over to Jesus Christ, he found the most stable basis for building an identity as a child of God, and he developed a security based on his personal worth before the Lord, rather than on what he was doing. As a result he had less and less need to try to reassure himself through the wheeler-dealer life style. This in turn helped his wife to be more trusting, and the destructive cycle operating in their marriage was reversed.

The Drive of an Underlying Fear

A song the Beatles made popular a few years ago expresses very poignantly the depth of the underlying fear that was driving Bob, and is driving many people: the fear of not being a worthwhile person. It also reveals that a person caught up in this fear uses all sorts of mechanisms in an attempt to compensate, as Bob did. Such a person is unable to see others, because he is too caught up in himself.

The Beatles' song describes "a real nowhere man" who sits in "nowhere land," occupied with "all his nowhere plans for nobody." The nowhere man, the song says, has no point of view. He does not really believe anything. He doesn't know where he's going. Yet, he is a self-important type of individual who cannot recognize the personhood of others around him. The song implies that all of us have some of the traits of the nowhere man. Though he seems to think he is important, the nowhere man usually suffers from a deep sense of worthlessness.

There are many people who carry this feeling that they are just not of value. But the reactions to this are often not so passive as the song implies. Nor are they always along the lines of Bob's attempts to impress. Sometimes the reactions to this feeling of unworthiness are quite angry and hostile.

Gene Davis was a 17-year-old boy who was so afraid of failure and so afraid of not living up to his parents' expectations that he became rebellious and sullen. He had the feeling that no matter what he did, it would not be acceptable. He expected rejection and was already angry at his parents before they opened their mouths. He anticipated that they would say something destructive, which they often did.

Gene's father was proud of the fact that he had operated his own business at age 13, and had always worked very hard. He compared his son unfavorably with himself and was extremely critical of the boy. He called Gene a "sissy" because his hair was long (when in fact it did not come over his ears). Mr. Davis frequently told his son, "You are going to be a failure," and made other similar prophecies of doom.

The mother often would break into tears and make some guilt-provoking statement whenever Gene would try to describe how he felt. She would say, "How can you feel that way?" Or, "Don't you realize what you are doing to your father and me?"

The more the boy felt rejected, the angrier he became and the poorer he performed. And the less well he performed, the more they tended to reject and condemn him. Thus the family was locked into a self-perpetuating destructive cycle.

In my counseling, I pointed out to Gene that he needed to recognize that he was created in God's image, that in God's eyes he was of great importance and could be correctly related to God through Jesus Christ. While I showed him this commitment would bring new meaning and order in his life, I did not imply that all his problems would be over. He would simply have a solid base on which to build. He would have new capacities and new motivations, and could begin to behave in a more responsible way, which would include obeying his parents. He would find a new sense of self-esteem and value.

As I dealt with Mr. and Mrs. Davis, I showed how they could interrupt the cycle if they would begin living the volitional love described in 1 Corinthians 13 and discussed in chapter 6 of this book. The parents needed to stop the double-checking, the doubt, the prophecies of doom, and all the other little things they were doing that tended to reject and belittle Gene. I counseled them to get off the unnecessary battlefields but be firm and consistent on important issues. I urged them to look for attributes for which to praise Gene, and to relate to him other than at times of crisis.

Unfortunately, like many other people, neither Gene nor his parents would take the necessary steps to reverse their downward cycle. They were so bitter and resentful that they were more anxious to win a battle or prove a point than they were to improve the relationship.

In some respects it is harder for parents in this type situation to alter their attitudes. Their children's behavior may be so blatantly destructive that they ignore the more subtle ways in which *they too* are destructive.

Guaranteeing Rejection
People who lack an adequate sense of worth may also get caught in another vicious trap. A person would rather be rejected for what he *does* than

for who he *is*. Many people who lack a sense of worth, and who therefore anticipate that they will not be accepted, exhibit unacceptable behavior so that the rejection will not hurt so much.

There are many complex interactions that bring about anticipated rejection. The person who feels of little value is responsible for his actions and cannot legitimately blame his actions on others, regardless of how much they may put him down. He could interrupt the cycle by stopping his behavior that provokes rejection. But on the other hand, friends, parents, and teachers may overreact to the negative side of the person and constantly criticize or belittle him, thus helping to spin the downward cycle.

A person may anticipate rejection for many reasons. It may be partly related to his childhood—the rejection he felt from one or both parents. Maybe he was constantly put down by other children or by teachers, or maybe he was unduly sensitive.

It is very difficult when dealing with people such as this to get them to even take the risk of playing it straight, or of beginning to act responsibly. The anticipation of rejection is so strong that the person has developed a formidable protection mechanism. He adopts a chaotic or very unconventional lifestyle and never really tries very hard. Then when he is rejected, it is because of his behavior. He won't have to face the awful possibility that he might have been rejected because of *who* he is, which is what he feared in the first place. You see, if he really tried, and then failed or was rejected, it would be intolerable for his basic self-concept.

Many of the young people in their mid and late teens at a psychiatric hospital where I was staff psychiatrist exhibited behavior which almost seemed designed to provoke rejection. And underneath we'd find a person who really assumed that there is no love out there, that there is no acceptance out there, that he is not of value.

Of course, there are varying degrees of this provocative life-style. Not all who feel little sense of personal worth are totally incapacitated.

Ralph was a man who had experienced a great deal of rejection as a youngster. His father in a drunken violent rage once tried to kill Ralph, and he generally grew up without receiving any love.

After he married, Ralph had a great deal of difficulty in accepting or loving his wife, or trusting her. He developed a very resentful and bitter attitude toward the whole world. He felt that everyone had something up his sleeve. Because his attitude was one of distrust, of being on guard, of being rather cynical, people responded to him negatively, which proved to him the world was a hostile place.

Such a person gets caught up in a self-fulfilling prophecy. He feels or believes that he will be rejected, and he develops a life style that in fact guarantees it. This results in increasing bitterness and lack of feeling worthwhile either to others or to himself.

The Need for Values

This is a very powerful need we have—to feel that we are valuable, that we are worthwhile. And to feel of worth, we need to live, as consistently as possible, a moral constructive life so that we and others recognize our value. But in order to live like this, we need a basic identity which assures us we are OK. And we need to know that there are ethics and values on which we can rely. As we shall see shortly, there is no answer to this need outside of an infinite, personal God who reveals Himself to us.

The problem one immediately confronts concerning ethics and values is: *What values shall I follow?* If one lives in a world in which the things that are true today are not true tomorrow, how does one ever know what is true at the moment?

We live in a time when mankind is afflicted with a sort of gray sickness. Instead of perceiving any clear moral blacks and whites, people see issues in 99 shades of gray. Everything is relative. There are no absolutes; there are no values that are eternal. Often along with this goes a sick permissiveness. As a result, many young people are given no adequate guidelines—neither by parents, by educators, by the church, nor by anyone else. No wonder they are often lost in a gray fog.

Mary was a victim of this gray sickness. Mary started early with sexual promiscuity. Since she was readily "available," most of the boys who went with her were primarily interested in sex, and Mary came to feel that was about all she had to offer.

As time went on, most of her relationships with boys and then with men were characterized by superficiality and heavily involved sex. Rather than helping relationships to be deeper and more meaningful as is sometimes claimed for premarital sex, it always kept them on a superficial level. When problems or anxieties developed, or when a relationship seemed threatened, Mary looked to sexual relations for an answer rather than dealing with the real problems. This is one of the reasons premarital sex is destructive. It forces the relationship more and more to be centered around the excitement of the act and less and less on developing the relationship of the two people.

Not surprisingly, Mary developed a deep sense of worthlessness, and she was very prone to anxiety. One cannot live successfully without a sense of worth. And one cannot have a well-developed sense of worth without definite moral and ethical standards. Those who would say that Mary just had too severe a conscience or was too uptight about morality reveal their abysmal ignorance of who we are.

Like Mary, many people are sinking in this gray society, because they have no real values or beliefs that they can express and follow. Not developing a sense of being valuable and worthwhile, they develop all sorts of reactions to their lack. These reactions vary from being a con man, a manipulator, or a rebel, to passively giving up.

The Source of Values

Today, many mental health professionals are recognizing the tremendous need for a person to feel worthwhile and are encouraging their patients and clients to behave responsibly and to follow good values. However, most counselors are totally unable to say where these values come from.

C. S. Lewis points out this dilemma in his book *The Abolition of Man* (Macmillan, New York, N.Y.): "In a sort of ghastly simplicity, we remove the organ and demand the function. . . . We castrate, and bid the geldings be fruitful."

God has revealed His standard of values to us through the Bible (the written Word) and through Jesus Christ (the living Word). Only a knowledge of the Word of God can give us eternal values that are good and right to follow and that do not change from year to year. Only Jesus Christ can give us the motivation and power to follow these principles, plus forgiveness and relief from guilt when we fail.

As we discussed on page 68, Christianity has sometimes been charged with contributing to man's poor self-image. And it is undeniably true that the Christian doctrines of the universal sinfulness of man, the ineffable glory of God, and the crucial importance of humbly turning oneself over to God have sometimes been twisted in such a way as to degrade man and destroy his sense of worth.

However, the Bible is simply honest about the plight of man. *All have* sinned and come short of the glory of God. *Each has* gone his own way. But instead of feeling guilty or put down, a person needs to admit this fact about himself and accept the forgiveness, cleansing, and healing that God offers him in Jesus Chris.. Then he will have a much greater chance of functioning as God designed him, and God designed man to be only slightly lower than the angels in this life, to love Him and each other.

God also designed us to be obedient to Him, and we cannot feel of value at the deepest level unless we *have confessed* our basic sin of self-centeredness and *continue* to confess our shortcomings, resting assured of His forgiveness, and then more obediently turning ourselves over to Him. When we do this, we are functioning as children of God, as members of His family, and this is what He intended for us in the first place.

God's Estimation of Our Worth

In the New Testament, Jesus emphatically taught His disciples that they were of personal worth and importance to God. He said, "What is the price of five sparrows? A couple of pennies? Not much more than that. Yet, God does not forget a single one of them. And He knows the number of hairs on your head. Never fear, you are far more valuable to Him than a whole flock of sparrows" (Luke 12:6, 7).

Too many people close their ears to God and thus have never heard Him saying those words to them: "You are far more valuable (to Me)!"

The tremendous importance of our having a sense of our own worth is emphasized in Paul's epistle to the Ephesians. He indicated that he was praying earnestly that those who knew Christ would also come to understand their own value in the sight of God. He writes, "I want you to realize that *God has been made rich* because we who are Christ's have been given to Him" (Eph. 1:18).

A great many people cannot accept the idea that God is enriched by having *them*. They feel they are worthless, good for nothing, of little value to themselves or others, much less to Almighty God.

Some may also object that the idea that we are worth a lot to God is contrary to proper Christian humility and denigrating to the glory of God. But why should we think the only way to glorify God is to debase man? Does He become more if we make ourselves less? That is a neurotic concept of man's humility and God's glory.

We can ordinarily judge the value of anything by the price that a knowledgeable person places upon it. By that criterion, man is the most valuable creation in the universe, for God valued man enough to pay the price of the infinite suffering of the cross for him.

At this point, we are once again confronted with the relevance of Christianity to mental health. As we said, the person who has problems with his self-image and feels of little worth anticipates rejection, tries to impress, becomes hostile, or behaves in other destructive ways. But the person who has really and truly found Jesus Christ can answer this identity question in a positive manner. "I am a joint heir with Jesus Christ. I am a son of God. I am tremendously important in the sight of God. Christ died for me, and I am acceptable to Him. He is living within me. We have a union, a relationship. There are also values, principles, ethics that I can count on. I can follow them. They work."

Society in general does not and perhaps never will agree with biblical morality. Today the disagreement is more marked than ever before in our lifetime. However, regardless of what kick society happens to be on, the values, principles, ethics, and morality of Scripture do not change. They represent reality. And a person who follows these does not just *feel* of value; he *is* of value.

A Positive Cycle

Thus, the vicious cycle of poor self-image, which prompts unacceptable behavior, which invokes a negative reaction from society, which further assaults the self-image is broken. It is replaced by a wonderful, contrasting, positive cycle. The good new self-image (a child of God) expresses itself in constructive behavior, which is more likely to bring a positive reaction from society, which further strengthens the person's concept that he is a worthwhile, valuable person.

But this positive self-image is not automatic for every Christian. Marie was definitely a Christian and had been for years. Yet her poor sense of personal worth led her into relying more and more on what others thought and less and less on being led of God.

Marie had married a man from a higher economic and educational class than herself. She needed very much to feel accepted and important, but she sensed that her husband's family viewed her as inferior.

This became a problem buried deep within that nagged at her. She became sensitive to what other people thought of her and constantly tuned in to whether they seemed to think she was worthwhile or of value. If she did not get the reassurance and praise she wanted, she felt threatened and resentful.

Finally she got into a situation in which she received criticism, probably unjustly. It built and built inside her until she was convinced there was a terrible plot to defame her, to ruin her reputation. Thus she ultimately became irrational—psychotic. One can see from this the terribly destructive effects of bitterness and resentment, and our need to base our identity on God rather than on what other people think.

Marie required medication to restore her capability for rational thought. Complete healing came only as she learned to appropriate her birthright as a Christian, an heir of God—which is a class far above any human nobility or station, and to forgive and seek forgiveness as was appropriate.

The Christian who has an inadequate sense of personal worth should pray, and should claim by faith the position of dignity and worth assigned him by God. He will become more and more aware of his uniqueness and his gifts (see chapter 11), and as he uses his gifts for the Lord in serving others, he will feel fulfilled as a person of value.

8

Building Roads to Nowhere

An irrepressible need of man is to have purpose. Brilliant men from atheists to Christians have described this need.

George Bernard Shaw said, "Every man is ill at ease until he has found his niche."

The equally brilliant, caustic, and ultimately psychotic Friedrich Nietzsche said, "He who has a *why* to live can bear almost any *how*."

Dietrich Bonhoeffer, when he was in a Nazi prison and was destined to be hanged one year later, made this statement, "In view of our supreme purpose, the present difficulties and disappointments seem trivial."

In other words, it's really not external circumstances that get people down. It's their belief that there is no meaning and purpose to what they are doing. This is a powerful truth. We can put up with anything if we believe there is meaning and purpose to it.

Victor Frankl, who quotes Nietzsche in his book, *Man's Search for Meaning* (Washington Square Press, New York, N.Y.), proved the truth of

Nietzsche's statement in the crucible of a Nazi concentration camp.

Frankl lost his wife, father, mother, and brother in the camps, was stripped of all his possessions and was reduced almost to the status of an animal.

In such conditions, Frankl faced the excruciating question whether life really had any meaning at all. He wrote, "The question which beset me was, 'Has all this suffering, this dying around us a meaning? For if not, then ultimately there is no meaning to survival; for a life whose meaning depends upon such a happenstance—whether one escapes or not —ultimately would not be worth living at all!'"

From his own experience and from observing the other prisoners, Frankl came to the conclusion that what matters most in life is the attitude one takes toward his life and circumstances. Some people were able to survive conditions that destroyed others. Why? Because they somehow found hope and a sense of meaning and purpose.

At the end of 1972 the Department of Health, Education, and Welfare of the United States Government released a massive study titled "Work in America." It warned that workers' boredom and dissatisfaction with their jobs was a serious and increasing threat to the American economy and to the nation.

The report recommended broad changes in American industry to provide "job enrichment," to give workers a new sense of meaning and purpose (and thereby increase their interest and productivity).

"Job enrichment" by European car makers, Volvo and Saab, involves having work teams assemble complete units of automobiles instead of repeating monotonous assembly line movements.

Many American companies have launched job enrichment programs also.

"Work in America" simply substantiates the fact that people need meaning and purpose in their work and in their lives, and that everything deteriorates without it. However, there is a much more serious and deeper crisis involving meaning and purpose than is reflected in American work conditions, important as these may be. There is a profound erosion of the very basis on which to find meaning and purpose.

Erich Fromm, who is strictly anti-Christian, has made an interesting comment in his book, *Escape From Freedom.* He points out that many people who, as he views it, have escaped the old authoritarianism of Scripture and religion and are free, surprisingly are floundering with their newfound freedom and seem bored, neurotic, and restless. Fromm can't isolate the basic problem here or explain how to get out of it, but he pinpoints the condition.

No Basis for Purpose

Innumerable writers, then, have pointed out this tremendous need for meaning and purpose in life. However, many are unable to say *how to find it.*

Stuart Babbage, in his book the *Vacuum of Unbelief,* says that modern higher education has cast out of its students the devils of darkness, superstition, ignorance, and error, but has given nothing adequate to take their place. He likens this to a parable of Jesus concerning a man who had a demon cast out, and nothing took its place. The house was swept clean, and the demon returned to find the house empty and readily accessible. Not only did this demon come back, but he brought seven others with him. And the end state was worse than the beginning (see Matt. 12:43-45).

Unfortunately, this parable seems prophetic of our day. We have taken the view that there is not an infinite, personal God who has revealed Himself to us. We have relegated truth and morality to the level of feelings, making them subjective and relative. And, while we have cast out some demons of ignorance and superstition, we are left with a vacuum of unbelief that is devastating the lives of many people, resulting in meaninglessness and purposelessness.

This attitude of meaninglessness is prevalent in many contemporary songs. When I was a teenager, about the most sophisticiated popular song had to do with, "What will I do when you are far away and I am blue; what'll I do?" Many songs today are raising powerful philosophical questions about the meaning of life, or they are reacting to the lack of meaning, sometimes whimsically, sometimes angrily. One song compares people with clouds hanging in the sky. Both people and clouds seem to constitute only big unanswered questions so far as their purpose or destiny is concerned. Eventually, like some clouds, a person will dissipate into nothingness, leaving behind only the question of what meaning, if any, his life had.

Another song describes the same feeling of meaninglessness. It repeats hello four times, then repeats good-bye four times, suggesting that life is nothing more than that. The song goes on to graphically symbolize this futility; it describes leaves turning from green to brown, withering with the wind, and crumbling to nothing in one's hand.

The same author has written another song which says that not only is there no meaning and purpose, but there is no way out. You are hopelessly conditioned. From the instant of your birth until the moment of your death, life consists of predetermined patterns as surely as breath must follow breath. There is no way of escape, and things will never change. Like a rat in a maze, you are doomed to grope your way through life to nowhere.

The profound cry for meaning observable in contemporary songs is also observable in some of the world's most ancient poetry. The biblical book of Ecclesiastes begins, "In my opinion, nothing is worthwhile; everything is futile" (1:2), and it comes back to this basic observation again and again. The poet details his many attempts to find meaning in life and bewails the agonizing result: "But as I looked at everything I had tried, it was all so useless, a chasing of the wind, and there was nothing really worthwhile anywhere" (2:11).

The effect of this debilitating philosophy of futility is also clearly expressed: "Everything is unutterably weary and tiresome" (1:8). Thus, this biblical poem, which views life "under the sun" or without regard for its spiritual dimension, exhibits remarkable similarity to the despair of today's secular society.

Donald Krill quotes Merton's use of a Greek word *anomie* to describe our current problems (*Existential Psychotherapy and the Problem of Anomie*, Social Work, Volume 14, Number 2, April 1969). The Greek word means *without law*. It does not refer to law-breaking but rather describes trying to live as if there are no absolute principles or concepts to follow. People are floundering in this *anomic* environment. It leaves unsatisfied their tremendous need to have meaning and purpose in life.

Second Thoughts

In 1973, *Time* magazine ran a special series of articles entitled "Second Thoughts About Man." This series reported a growing uneasiness among intellectuals that there is more to man than some have thought, that we are missing something. According to *Time,* "The original optimism that man could start exclusively with himself and learn all that he needs to know is giving way to doubt, frustration, and often despair."

A few selected quotes give the general idea:

"By whatever name, there is an impending sense of change in the world of ideas. The reigning wisdom that informed and compelled the past few decades is under attack or, at the very least, under cross-examination. That wisdom has been variously called liberalism, rationalism, scientism: concepts certainly not identical but related. But now man's confidence in his power to control his world is at a low ebb. Technology is seen as a dangerous ally, and progress is suspect. Even the evolutionists share this unease. Their hope lies not in man as he is but in some mutant superman."

"The physical world became the domain of western science, though man sometimes seems less the master of that world than its mechanic."

"At the heart of the ferment of the '70s is a deep, even humble, perception that man and his universe are more complex than he recently thought."

"Some scientists themselves (realize) that they have fewer answers than they once believed."

"There is a sneaking reappearance of the old notion that certain fixed elements in man (once unscientifically known as human nature) are not susceptible to environmental changes."

Many social and physical scientists, in their honesty, are now openly talking about the fact that there seems to be more to man and his universe than determinists have believed. However, as long as any investigator, no matter how brilliant, is operating on the basic assumption that man himself represents the highest form of intelligence and there is no infinite and personal God who has revealed truth to man, it will be impossible for him to come to definite answers.

The Source of Purpose

Ironically, as many of these brilliant men struggle with the problem about "human nature," the Bible has already given the answers. The "sneaking reappearance of the old notion that certain fixed elements in man are not susceptible to environmental changes" may well reflect a vague awareness of the truth the Bible has given us about man: that he is created in the image of God, and no matter how rudimentary those vestiges are, they are there and fixed. And man will never feel fulfilled or reach his maximal potential until those qualities have a growing, developing expression. As a man, Jesus Christ is the only person who has ever fully lived as He was designed. Created in the image of God as a man, He fully expressed God. "The Father and I are one; I only do what the Father wills," He said (see John 8:29; 10:30).

A Christian has the Holy Spirit within, and He continually nudges us to give up our egocentricity and allow the power and life of Christ to flow through us more and more. This is what brings man to his highest fulfillment. No mutation will ever produce the desired man the evolutionists are seeking. Only the new birth and the power of the Holy Spirit within can lead man toward his rightful destiny, which Romans 8:29 tells us is to be conformed to the image of Christ.

But man resists this idea. In his pride, ·man wants to believe he is the highest intelligence. He is the "captain of his ship." He alone can and will call the shots. Man will sometimes accept the concept of an impersonal God or force. He will accept a vague, virtually pantheistic notion of a spirit within the universe, but he exhibits an intrinsic rebellion against the concept of a personal God who has actually walked this earth in the person of Jesus Christ.

The personal God who offers man the free gift of salvation is offensive to our egocentricity. We would rather believe that we are already "God," that all we need to do is allow the God within us to come out. Or we simply ignore that there is any God at all.

Not only is the free gift of salvation offensive, but the idea that one must make a choice is equally offensive. One must either accept or refuse a proffered gift. This means one either has it or he doesn't.

Today, there is also an immediate resistance against the notion that there is knowable, final truth that one is responsible for accepting or rejecting. It is much more palatable to believe truth is relative; every man must decide for himself; and whatever he decides is OK.

But this leads to a great vacuum of unbelief, because there *is* a way to ultimate truth, to God, and it is through Jesus Christ, who said, "I am the way, the truth, and the life; no man cometh unto the Father but by Me" (John 14:6, KJV).

Kinky Substitutes

So people begin to try to fill the vacuum, to find some meaning somewhere. This is, no doubt, a most powerful dynamic behind drug abuse. Many drugs *chemically* evoke the feeling of "oneness with the universe," of great camaraderie. People will report that on drugs they feel great love toward their fellow man. The truth is they are often off in the corner doing their own thing, having no intelligent interaction with anyone. But the *feeling* is of great love, great camaraderie.

People on LSD have had ecstatic experiences. Supposedly they have tapped into the source of the universe and have had tremendous truths revealed to them. In laboratory experiments, those given LSD have been asked to write down the truths they have received, and what do they write? Some of the most trite, mundane truisms you would ever expect to see!

However, the false feeling of tremendous oneness with the universe, of finally coming to the source of all truth, has immense appeal because of this great need for meaning. Nor does this stop with the people on pot or LSD. One-fourth of all prescriptions written by the medical profession in this country are for mind or mood-altering drugs! And, of course, the people who use illegal drugs are a drop in the bucket compared to the six to nine million alcoholics who exist in the country today.

We learned in elementary science that nature abhors a vacuum The soul, the human spirit, also abhors a vacuum. And that vacuum, that need for meaning, will be filled with something, or a person will look for various ways to escape the haunting spectre of meaninglessness.

Promiscuity

Some people go the drug route. Others go the sex route. Behind the promiscuous sex of today is something more than the permissive environment in which we live. There is a tremendous focus today on feelings as if they were the only reality. So anything that gives a powerful feeling of love, closeness, or meaning is all that many people can hope for. Sexual relations often supply this, at least momentarily.

This emphasis on feeling, aided and abetted by TV commercials and the mind-boggling brain washing that comes from advertising in general has oriented us toward assuming that instant everything is the necessary norm. It's your inalienable right never to smell bad, never to have sluggish bowels, have trouble sleeping, be nervous, be unpopular, be less than a sexpot, or have the wet look. There is something in a spray or a pill or a bottle that will bring instant correction. Anything short of instant delight is intolerable, and if that isn't your experience, you are just not using the right toothpaste, spray, gargle, gunk, goo, or gadget. In this kind of instant-everything milieu, there is a powerful tendency to try to find instant relationships, warmth, and acceptance. Sex is often the vehicle by which people try to obtain this.

Of course, these devices may temporarily or partially meet one's need for meaning, but they don't completely meet it. So there becomes a "driven" quality to the person's life. One has to grasp at all the fulfillment one can get, even partially, because one never has adequate fulfillment.

This is characteristic of all neurotic behavior which, by my definition, is *an attempt to get certain needs met by mechanisms which are partially but never totally successful.* This is why neuroses become self-perpetuating.

Marge was married to a rather self-righteous man who often related to her as a father or as one who needed to instruct or advise her. He also was very much involved in a local church and tended to preach to his wife, or at least to use Scripture or religious ideals to back up his criticism and instruction of her. For some years, raising her children gave her purposeful interests, but as the children grew older, she found her life increasingly meaningless. She did not have a growing personal relationship with Jesus Christ, and her relationship with her husband was not meaningful.

Marge first tried to find meaning by identifying with people much younger than herself and by having an affair with one of them. Ultimately that brought only shame and depression. After getting over that somewhat, she began to seek meaning in the occult. She became obsessed with books about astrology and ESP, and finally drifted into spiritism.

The Occult

Recent times have seen a veritable revolution relating to increasing interest and involvement in the occult. This fascination and involvement manifests itself in an outpouring of children's games that deal with this, in increasing usage of horoscopes, astrology, mediumistic activity, spiritism, spiritualism, so-called white magic, black magic, satanism, and Eastern mysticism. Movement into these areas represents a desperate search for some meaning, some significance beyond being a mechanistic man. Opening these doors to the occult is an open invitation to satanic influence and control.

Ben got interested in spiritualism while attending college. He became intrigued with reincarnation and associated himself with fortunetellers. Sometimes something seemed to take over his faculties, causing him to engage in automatic writing. The messages at first were quite encouraging. However, they became more and more accusatory. Finally Ben was hearing voices and generally appeared out of contact with reality.

A minister referred Ben to some Christians who were involved in a ministry of deliverance. A dramatic exorcism took place, and the demons that had come into him via the open door of the occult were cast out. He then received Jesus Christ, who filled the vacuum in his life. No longer did Satan have control of him, nor did he any longer experience the phenomenon of automatic writing. He was now in touch with ultimate reality; which reflected itself in a return to the reality about him so that he could function normally.

However, Ben developed a problem secondary to this traumatic experience that is common to many who have seen the power of Satan and experienced deliverance. He began to feel that any time he had any kind of physical or mental symptom, it was the work of some demon. Finally demons were lurking behind every rock and around every corner. Relief for this came as he got his eyes off Satan and claimed the centrality of Jesus Christ as Lord, focusing on the Victor rather than on the enemy, and being willing to take personal responsibility for himself rather than immediately pawning everything off on Satan. It was C. S. Lewis who said in *Screwtape Letters* that two things Satan likes people to do is either to make a joke out of him or become obsessed with him.

A Cause

While some people use drugs or sex or the occult as a neurotic mechanism, other people try to fill their vacuum with violence or with violently espousing some cause. As long as such a person has a cause in which to invest powerful emotions and has a group that is solidly behind that cause, he has a definite sense of meaning and purpose. The dynamics of the group together serving the cause is actually more important than winning the cause. It is the emotional steam of the group working together to accomplish something that gives the sense of meaning and purpose.

Sociological studies after World War 2 showed that some people who were fully committed to the Nazi cause became equally powerfully committed to the Communist cause. It was not the philosophy that was most important to the person, though he'd die for it. But the crucial thing was being in a powerful cause.

Relativity

John Dewey is renowned for his statement, "Absolutely no absolutes." Origins of this philosophy can be traced back long before Dewey. At any rate, we have sown the wind of relativity and are reaping the whirlwind of meaninglessness as the result of carrying that philosophy to its logical conclusion.

The forces of humanism, rationalism, naturalism, and materialism with their antisupernatural bias pervade all secular education and, irony of ironies, even pervade some seminaries. There is no hope of finding meaning and purpose within the framework of this philosophy. Many people are trapped in this system, one they themselves have devised. If it's really true that there is no infinite and personal God who has revealed Himself and His absolute truths, if what's true today will not be true tomorrow, then we are reduced to being animals, or, even worse, machines. Each man *is* an island. We are meaningless creatures who crawl about and do our thing, but there is no ultimate purpose to any of it.

A Sublime Alternative

Within this framework, a person becomes a robot, a machine, a gear, a cog. But man was not made to be part of blind, meaningless machinery. Even the person who believes in a mechanistic view cannot tolerate it. And so we see today a movement away from the machine concept: men become romantics, mystics, gurus, clairvoyants. The good news of Scripture is that there is a third alternative. A person can become a real man, a complete human being through the grace of God. In other words, he can become a Christian.

Man's need for meaning in life again spotlights the relevance, indeed the desperate importance of Jesus Christ, for apart from Him a person's whole relationship with God is disordered. He suffers an alienation, a separation that makes it extraordinarily difficult to find valid meaning and purpose.

Fortunate is the person who has experienced and who knows: *I belong to God. Jesus Christ is alive and His Spirit lives within me. An exciting process has begun that makes it possible for me to reach my rightful destiny and be fulfilled as one created in the image of God. I am a person of extreme value to God. Even the hairs on my head are numbered; I am a unique person, uniquely created by God for a unique purpose, and I have a unique sphere of influence.*

Each of us does have a unique sphere of influence. Of course, there is a great deal of overlap from one person to the next, but each has his own sphere. Words, deeds, circumstances take on a new hue and importance, because we really do influence others.

Trials, disappointments, frustrations do not have to defeat us, because nothing is without its purpose as we are following God. Anything that comes our way is an opportunity to experience that the Lord's grace is sufficient, as Paul says, and there are no exceptions to this (see 2 Cor. 12:9). Everything that happens to us can result in growth, development, and reaching others. This brings meaning and purpose to every aspect of our lives.

The Apostle Paul labored indefatigably, and turned his world upside down for Christ, though he endured all kinds of privation to do so. Why? Because he had a supreme purpose. He had a why to live, and the how was incidental.

Paul wrote, "I have learned how to get along happily whether I have much or little. I know how to live on almost nothing or with everything. I have learned the secret of contentment in every situation, whether it be a full stomach or hunger, plenty or want, for I can do everything God asks me to do with the help of Christ who gives me the strength and power" (Phil. 4:11-13).

Paul could make such a statement, and an equally radical statement such as, "In all things give thanks" (1 Thes. 5:18), because he knew everything had a purpose and would ultimately work together for good in his life. Because absolute total victory will ultimately come to us through the resurrection, he could say at the end of his powerful passage on the resurrection, "Therefore . . . be ye steadfast, unmovable, always abounding in the work of the Lord, forasmuch as ye know that your labor is not in vain in the Lord" (1 Cor. 15:58, KJV).

All of these powerful principles give us the potential as Christians to find increasing meaning and purpose, but by no means is all this automatically ours simply by virtue of our being Christians. We have a new base to build upon, and new motivations and new capacities. But we are engaged in a perpetual spiritual warfare that pits our original egocentricity and the powers of hell against the Holy Spirit within us.

Teachings that imply *automatic* victory for the Christian simply through making a commitment to Christ do terrible disservice to His cause because they omit the reality of the spiritual warfare and the power of our egocentricity. The simple honest fact is that the Christian life involves a great deal of struggle as well as rest in Christ, painful growth as well as joyous growth, suffering as well as marvelous healing, disrupted relationships as well as wonderful new relationships in the body of Christ, the fellowship of believers.

But despite all this, overwhelming victory is ours through Christ, who loved us enough to die for us. "For I am convinced that nothing can ever separate us from His love. Death can't, and life can't. The angels won't, and all the powers of hell itself cannot keep God's love away. Our fears for today, our worries about tomorrow, or where we are—high above the sky, or in the deepest ocean —nothing will ever be able to separate us from the love of God demonstrated by our Lord Jesus Christ when He died for us" (Rom. 8:38, 39).

Part IV

How Are Our Needs Met?

9

To Have and To Hassle

The earliest and most crucial arena where our needs are first met, or not met, is the home. The patterns established there influence us the rest of our lives. And the most crucial relationship in the home is that between husband and wife.

The Bible clearly teaches that the home was established by God. It also reveals to us the proper roles of husband, wife, and children in the home. When relationships with God are right, and husband, wife, and children are functioning as God intended, the family meets the basic needs of its members for giving and receiving love and for feeling of value, and it provides a foundation for finding meaning and purpose.

However, the family today is under tremendous attack. There are many who project that the home as we know it is on the way out: that relationships will become even more casual and transient than they are now and that some new structure will be devised for rearing children.

Of course, to some degree, this is already taking place. Divorce rates rise higher and higher, and we see more and more people trying to order their lives as if the Bible were not true. Those who do not build on the base of God's revealed truth tend to conclude that whatever the majority is doing is "right." Therefore, they are easily seduced or intimidated by whatever destructive fad society at large may be pursuing.

The Divine Plan

But what does the Word of God say? In the first place, I believe it is highly significant that of all the metaphors God could have chosen to describe the relationship between Himself and His people, He chose the relationship of husband to wife, or bridegroom to bride. Isaiah 54:5 says, "For your Creator will be your 'husband'; The Lord of hosts is His name: He is your Redeemer, the Holy One of Israel, the God of all the earth."

When Adam was confronted with Eve, he said, " 'This is it . . . she is part of my own bone and flesh! Her name is *woman* because she was taken out of a man.' This explains why a man leaves his father and mother and is joined to his wife in such a way that the two become one person" (Gen. 2:23, 24).

Jesus elaborates on this theme in Mark 10:7-9. "For from the very first, He made man and woman to be joined together permanently in marriage. Therefore, a man is to leave his father and mother, and he and his wife are united so that they are no longer two but one, and no man may separate what God has joined together."

Because this relationship should exist as just described, Paul states in Ephesians, "You husbands show the same kind of love to your wives as Christ showed to the church when He died for her... (That the husband and wife are one body is proved by the Scripture which says, 'A man must leave his father and mother when he marries, so that he can be perfectly joined to his wife, and the two shall be one.') I know this is hard to understand, but it is an illustration of the way we are parts of the body of Christ. So again I say, a man must love his wife as a part of himself; and the wife must see to it that she deeply respects her husband—obeying, praising, and honoring him" (5:25, 31-33).

Both the Old and New Testaments reveal the great responsibility of parents to rear their children as unto the Lord. "O Israel, listen: Jehovah is our God, Jehovah alone. . . . You must think constantly about these commandments I am giving you today. You must teach them to your children and talk about them when you are at home or out for a walk; at bedtime and the first thing in the morning" (Deut. 6:4-7). "And now a word to you parents. Don't keep on scolding and nagging your children, making them angry and resentful. Rather, bring them up with the loving discipline the Lord Himself approves, with suggestions and godly advice" (Eph. 6:4). "Children, obey your parents. This is the right thing to do, because God has placed them in authority over you. Honor your father and mother" (Eph. 6:1, 2).

These Scriptures reveal the divine pattern for the home. The family is the structure through which God brings order, reveals love, and sets the stage for maximal growth, which comes by husbands, wives, and children relating to each other under God as He intended. If those in the home are functioning as designed, the home becomes therapeutic in a sense.

That is to say, after 15 years of living together,

a couple or family should be more fulfilled and more mature because of their interactions than they were after five years of living together. Our relationships should call forth the best from others. Tragically we often play games, operate in an egocentric fashion, and call forth the worst from others.

The next chapters chart a course for meeting one another's needs through living according to the design of God. At our counseling center, we see more husbands and wives in various stages of warfare than any other category of people seeking help. While egocentricity is always the ultimate root of problems between people, there are some profound differences between men and women that have a great deal to do with the warfare that takes place between the sexes.

Male-female differences exist for a number of reasons. For a husband and wife to reach maximum fulfillment, they must complement each other. Our egocentricity leads us to attempt to force other people to be molded in our image. Thus, many husbands and wives, rather than experiencing what it means for two to become one flesh, battle to change each other.

There is a trend today toward denying differences between the sexes. However, research has shown up examples of male-female differences even in infants. These findings are not 100% applicable, but they do show general trends and patterns. Therefore, regardless of the popularity of the unisex concept, there is more difference between men and women than in their plumbing arrangements. And if these differences are not understood, the relationship will never develop in accordance with the actual need.

Research Findings

Boy babies tend to cry more, sleep less, and smile less than girls. However, when confronted with stress, girls are more likely to cry, and boys are more likely to strike out in some way.

I have a beautiful picture of my son, Jim, when he was about 18 months of age. He had been in a playpen with rungs around it. The picture shows about five rungs strewn on the ground, and he is proudly, defiantly, toddling across the yard.

Girls respond more positively to touch and sound and pictures of faces. Boys respond more positively to geometric designs. Girl babies tend to collect their treasures, their playthings, and draw them close to themselves. Boys scatter them all over the room.

There are also some general differences between adult males and females. Some of these differences are obviously elaborations of those observed in infants. Of course, there are exceptions to these general masculine, feminine tendencies, and if you feel some of these exceptions apply to you, it does not mean there is something wrong with your masculinity or femininity. Nevertheless, these differences are generally applicable, and need to be understood.

Male Tendencies

Men tend to be more interested in events, things, logic, and the big picture. They are relatively less comfortable with and sensitive to the sharing of feelings. Their sexual expressions and feelings are more likely to be impulsive, reach a peak fast, be over fast, and be relatively less dependent on the overall relationship.

A man has a powerful emotional need to feel

respected, admired, and followed. He needs affirmation that he is more than adequate to meet the demands placed on him in every area of his life.

I see case after case of serious conflict between husband and wife, in which the husband gets very little sense of being respected, admired, or needed. Then at his office, he counsels one of his secretaries who is having marital problems. She looks up to him, respects him, admires him, can talk to him, and wishes so much that her own husband would talk to her and listen to her. He begins to respond to her admiration in such a way that he becomes more and more emotionally involved and ultimately sexually involved.

I see more cases of infidelity in this type situation than I do of someone who is simply looking for an extramarital sexual experience.

Female Tendencies

Females, in general, are more interested in people. The husband comes home and says the world is going to the dogs. People don't care any more. He goes into some theory, and the wife says, "Who did you have a hard time with today?"

Women are more tuned in to people, to the details surrounding a person.

"Didn't that woman at the market remind you of Aunt Maude?" she asks.

He says, "What woman?"

She says, "The one in the plaid coat."

"I didn't notice a woman in a plaid coat."

"It was the woman in the white shoes and carrying that cute little clutch purse."

"You're kidding! I'm supposed to notice what kind of purse some woman's carrying?"

But *she* notices.

Relatively, women operate more on an intuitive, feeling level. They tend to be more comfortable with the expression of feelings. Their sexual expressions are more likely to be an outgrowth of their overall relationship. They require a sense of communion, of closeness, of commitment, of affection in order to reach maximal sexual fulfillment. The whole sexual process develops slower than with the male.

Wives are sometimes dumbfounded that their husbands could be interested in sexual relations shortly after some argument. The tendency for wives, at that point, is to conclude "that's all he's interested in." But this interaction may simply reflect one of the differences that exists between the sexes.

The woman's most basic emotional need is to share meaningfully in another life, to be needed. Remember, Eve was created to be a helpmeet for Adam. The woman must feel needed, not in some utilitarian role as maid, or lover, or chauffeur, or baby-sitter, but in a life-sharing way as companion, friend, helpmate.

One of the most common complaints I hear is, "My husband doesn't really need me. He could hire a maid, take a mistress, and never miss me. He never talks to me. He's an owl, and I don't know anything about him. I never learn about anything that's going on until we have some people over to the house. He starts talking to someone, and I hear for the first time that he's been uptight about his business. I never know anything unless we have company, and that's why I invite people over, to find out what's going on."

The woman needs to feel that she is involved with a person and sharing life with this person.

With that background, let's identify the universal neuroses of women and men respectively.

The Feminine Neurosis

The universal fear of women is that they will be objects—used or abused—rather than really being cared for as persons. They fear being sexual objects, servants, those who take care of the house or of the children. They fear that they will be seemingly cared for a while and then abandoned, either emotionally or physically.

The Southern Appalachian folk song "Black-eyed Susie" reveals the female resentment of being used as an object:

"Hey, old man, I want your daughter
To cook my food and carry my water.

. . . .

I asked Miss Susie to be my wife;
She come at me with a Barlow knife."

Another Southern folk song, "Single Girls," further reflects a lament of the female neurosis:

"When I was a single girl, I went to
the store to buy.
Now I am a married girl,
I just rock that cradle and cry.
I wish I was a single girl again."

One of the more common statements I hear is, "The one thing my husband is interested in is going to bed and having sex. That's all he cares about." The husband doesn't say that, and there may be a great deal of evidence that he has a much deeper relationship than that with his wife. But this is her fear: "I'm not really being cared for; I'm just an object." And this is what is really behind many of the arguments between husbands and wives, whether or not it is recognized.

The Masculine Neurosis

Fear of being subjugated by a female is the universal masculine neurosis. Coupled with this is the fear of being weighed in the balance and found wanting—inadequate—in some or all of his roles.

The folk song "The Bald-headed End of the Broom" speaks of the masculine neurosis:

"Boys, keep away from the girls, I say;
　　and give 'em lots of room;
'Cause when you're wed, they'll beat you till
　　you're dead
　　with the bald-headed end of the broom.
When married folks have lots of cash, then love
　　runs smooth
　　and strong;
But when they have to feed on hash, then love
　　don't last very long.
With a wife and 17 half-starved kids, I'm telling
　　you it's not very fun
When the butcher comes around with a bill to
　　collect and a dog and a double-barreled gun."

The Deadly Combination

If the wife does not feel loved, she will begin to try to draw her husband into her life in order to reassure herself that he cares, that he's involved. She may try to get his attention by talking about all the things around the house that need fixing. She may make various complaints about how she is feeling physically or mentally. She may begin to express great concern about the children, or she may begin to nag him about various traits she doesn't like, or complain that he is never home, and so forth.

All the man hears in all of this is that he is inadequate. She seems to be trying to subjugate him, to control him, and since this strikes at the heart of his basic neurosis, he resists. He pushes his wife away. He responds either with hostility or withdrawal. This in turn stimulates the wife to try that much harder to draw him in. Thus the vicious downward spiral continues.

Mr. Smith and his wife were middle-aged. He was a successful business executive. Their initial reason for coming to me was that the wife was finding herself becoming increasingly depressed, tense, and angry.

Mrs. Smith was aware of her beginning problems about a year prior to her coming to see me. During this time she had an illness that required her to be in bed. She developed mounting resentment over the fact that her husband continued to be extremely involved with all his activities. She began to feel more and more that he had abandoned her and that she would have to fend for herself. She decided she would go to work outside the home and be on her own. She had a sense of resentment toward her husband, and toward his business for taking so much of his time. She was also angry with her husband for being insensitive to the fact that she was very lonely.

In this setting, she began to focus on herself more and more. This caused her husband to see her as selfish and demanding. And since she *was* somewhat unreasonable, it made it easy for him to see the problem as only hers; he tended not to see the core of truth in her complaints.

He also tended to react to her demanding behavior by withholding the things she wanted. Otherwise he would seem to be a man who was being controlled, dominated by his wife.

As the Smiths were able to begin to focus on each other's needs rather than their own and made a commitment to meet each other's needs, the sense of criticism, bitterness, resentment, and passive withholding began to drop away. The wife became more certain of her husband's love and commitment to her, and many of the other issues that had been so frustrating simply vanished.

In the final analysis, almost every conflict that husbands and wives get into (possibly that anybody gets into) has to do with ego battles. We are fighting for our rights, our needs. Or we are trying to change the other person to conform to our specifications.

Concerning the latter, some women seem to be a bit more vulnerable to having "rescue fantasies" than men are. They marry a man, and their mission in life is to make him over in some way. This usually has disastrous results. Formula for failure: devote your life to remaking someone in your image or some image you have in your head of how he or she should be.

Many conflicts occur in marriage because both partners feel, *if only my partner were like me*. We settle into an "if only" attitude. "If only she wouldn't wear all that hardware in her hair when we go to bed. If only she would put the top back on the toothpaste tube just once. If only she didn't nag so much. If only she kept a better house. If only she were nicer to my friends."

And she says, "If only he would take me out once in a while. If only he would talk to me. If only he would quit drinking. If only he would go to church. If only he would mow the lawn."

So many people are caught up in an acute case of "if onlys," and there is very little help for a person so long as he or she focuses on what the other needs to do.

Both Sides Can Win

Ultimately, the war between the sexes can be resolved to the advantage of both sides when volitional love as described in 1 Corinthians 13 and in chapter 6 of this book is applied. This means shifting from a primary focus of worrying how you're going to get your needs met to considering how you can meet the other person's needs.

We need to develop Spirit-controlled eyes and ears so that we may especially attend to the other person's needs. In order to interrupt the interlocking masculine-feminine neuroses, the husband must become an *innovative initiator*. He should be the one to initiate communication, to initiate expressions of love, to initiate discipline in the home, to be on the lookout for things that need to be done around the home and to do them.

Husband, do you want to be head of your home? Jesus said, "To be the greatest, be a servant" (Matt. 23:11). Not the kind of servant who is subjugated, who takes orders. Jesus cited Himself as a model of serving others (Luke 22:27), and He took orders from no man. But husbands are to voluntarily serve the needs of their wives and the needs of their families.

Men, you can't have it both ways. You don't want your wife to be on your back? You don't want to be subjugated? Then you must take the initiative. Otherwise, she is certain to become anxious and to feel unloved. She will begin to try to get your attention, which you will tend to resist.

Let's see how this principle might work with a common problem—the battle of the garbage pail. The wife feels the least he could do is to take out the garbage. The husband is operating under the delusion that when he comes home from work, his responsibility is ended, and taking the garbage out is part of "woman's work."

Thus a war of nerves begins. Finally, the garbage pail is not only full but overflowing. Coffee grounds are descending to the floor, and fruit flies are hovering over banana peels as black as tar. Finally the wife explodes. She pours out all of her pent-up frustrations, stating that her husband never does anything, could not care less about her and the children, and is good for nothing around home but to read the paper and watch TV.

With that, he angrily grabs the pail, stomps out, and empties it. All the time he is feeling subjugated, belittled, and resentful. The wife, for her part, realizes he hardly emptied the garbage pail because of love for her. She knows she extracted that service from him, and feels equally horrible.

Now, imagine the same situation, except the husband has the strength to be an innovative initiator. The same garbage pail is nearly full. Without any words, he simply takes it out, empties it, washes it out, and brings it back. All the time he is doing this, he is operating from a position of strength. He does not feel subjugated. He does not feel put down. He does this unappealing task voluntarily, and it is a true gift to the wife.

She responds as one who has received a gift, because in this case she knows she did not manipulate or extract it from him. She feels more loved, more secure, and therefore has less tendency to nag or complain.

The husband should be the initiator in letting the wife in on his life. Wives are constantly complaining about how they have to dig and pick to find out what's going on with their husbands. The husbands resent the digging and picking. Obviously, the way to avoid this is to take the initiative in communication.

All of this is another way of saying what Ephesians 5:25 has already put forth. "Husbands love your wives even as Christ also loved the church, and gave Himself for it" (KJV). The wife needs to feel loved and secure. When the husband takes the initiative to express his caring, his loving, his involvement, he is in fact functioning as God intended, and this is what works. As soon as the husband thinks he has already loved his wife enough, he has gotten off the track. The love of Christ that we have been commanded to express to our wives is limitless.

Creative Affirmation

The wife can also play a healing role, as a *creative affirmer,* one who builds up and encourages her husband. She was made to be the helpmate. She is more intuitive, more aware of feelings, and is therefore uniquely designed to be the creative affirmer and responder.

I have had many wives tell me they are not about to be affirmative toward their husbands, because their husbands already think too much of themselves. Besides, if she took a positive attitude, he might think he's all right. He's still got a lot of changes to make as far as she is concerned. She wants to call these to his attention as often as possible. Of course, the man responds to this by either withdrawing or becoming more hostile.

We men have fragile egos and need a great deal of affirmation. Women often use their intuitive creative skills in affirming a man prior to marriage and then switch to the negative later. This tends to produce a hot war.

If a wife is going to bring healing into a relationship, she'll respond to the husband as the head of the home, will show respect for him, and follow him. When a husband has a wife who relates to him in this way, he finds it easier to share with her, and to take more and more responsibility as he feels less and less subject to being judged, put down, subjugated.

Usually, when Ephesians 5 is being discussed in a couples' Bible study, there is immediate focus on wives being submissive to husbands. Various jokes are made to hide some of the tension that develops over this idea, especially among the women. Less noticed but no less important in this passage is the command that husbands are to love their wives as Jesus Christ loved the church. My contention is that if husbands would love their wives in this way, being submissive would seldom be an issue.

I am only too well aware that simply saying husbands and wives should relate to each other in the ways I have described by no means solves the problem. These healing roles and relationships go against the grain of our natural reactions. So relating properly becomes a spiritual issue. Only as we begin to develop the mind of Christ, can we begin to be husbands and wives after the biblical model. We must learn what it means: "for to me to live is Christ," what it means to "die daily" to selfishness, to fighting for our rights, to being reactors. We need for the Lord to teach us to be Christians in the nitty-gritty relationships of the home.

Not long ago, I learned this lesson over a rather mundane issue. I like to get up early, make a pot of coffee, and study. About an hour later, I take Betsy a cup of coffee and awaken her. However, I had a pet peeve over finding the coffeepot with last night's grounds still in it. I would angrily wash it out, and later remind Betsy to do something about the situation. Finally I had enough negative charges attached to the coffeepot that I refused to clean it. As much as I like perked coffee, I would leave the pot dirty, make instant coffee, and carry this up to Betsy, who also prefers it perked. She would take a sip, look sheepishly at me, and say, "Was the pot dirty?"

This was, of course, the payoff question of the coffeepot game, and at this point I made the final move and said, "Again!"

Shortly after we had engaged on this battlefield, we were attending a pastors' conference at which I was speaking. While in the middle of speaking to them about interrupting destructive cycles and getting rid of the "if onlys," I was suddenly struck with my hypocrisy. Right then and there, I confessed the coffeepot battle, told my wife I loved her, and would commit myself to cleaning out the pot, regardless of its state.

An interesting thing has occurred. The pot is hardly ever dirty any more when I get to it in the morning. "So again I say, a man must love his wife as a part of himself, and the wife must see to it that she deeply respects her husband—obeying, praising, and honoring him" (Eph. 5:33).

A husband or a wife is on the right track and beginning to grow when he or she can read this verse of Scripture and immediately begin to think of how he or she can meet the needs of the other person in more and more creative ways. But the person who reads this passage and immediately reflects on what the other person ought to be doing is already going in the wrong direction.

After all, Ephesians 5 does not say: "Husbands, your wives should obey you; wives, your husbands should love you." What your mate should do is not your primary concern and is certainly not the focus of this passage. The question is, what kind of husband or wife are you?

10

"Have I Reached the Party to Whom I Am Speaking?"

One day I was sitting on my sofa busily preparing a talk on family life. My eight-year-old son, John, was sitting near me, chattering away. I was not really paying any attention to him and responded to his chatter with "uh-huh, uh-huh."

Finally I heard his voice trail off and get weak. I glanced up at him, and there he was, looking sad and rejected. Then it hit me! I was writing about how family members should relate to each other, but I was doing a strikingly poor job of it myself.

I put my work down and got eyeball to eyeball with him, and I said, "OK, John, tell me about it." John's face brightened and he told me all about his thing. He had received a great gift; I had listened!

Probably one of the most powerful actions for implying acceptance of someone is to listen. Many people have not developed the art of listening. You have probably talked to someone and suddenly realized he was looking through you, or around you, or was generally fidgety. Soon it became very obvious he was not listening but was waiting for the first pause so he could say his piece. Many parties, get-togethers, or so-called fellowships, whether over cocktails or cookies, are of this caliber. There is much talking, but no one is listening.

Some married couples have developed extreme non-listening attitudes. Elaine and George were such a couple. Whenever Elaine talked, George began to inspect the diplomas and pictures on my office wall, look out the window, and tap his feet on the floor.

Whenever George talked, Elaine appeared to be attentive, but she was in fact poised like a hundred-yard-dash man on the starting blocks, waiting to hear the gun that would send her off. For her, the gun sounded whenever George said anything that had some emotional charge attached to it that was painful to her. She would then immediately bring up his past shortcomings. At no point did she give any indication whatsoever that she was listening to what he was saying or understanding what he meant. She was actually warding off real or imagined threats to her by countering with some guilt-provoking accusation from the past.

Obviously, no true communication took place here. Each of them was engaged in what Paul Tournier has called "the dialogue of the deaf."

Many times, like Elaine, we do not actually listen to a person and try to understand what he or she means, but we simply react to some word that sends us off on our own associations and thoughts. We begin to formulate a comeback, to develop some speech of our own, and are no longer paying any attention to the person speaking.

The Advice-Giver

Some people are so primarily oriented toward giving advice that this also blocks listening. The person who needs a great deal of reassurance that he is useful and needed sometimes tries to meet this need by being the advice-giver, whether it is needed or not. It is no fun to talk to such people. You can see them poised, ready to pounce and tell you what you ought to do. And then they wonder why others don't like to talk with them.

A person may have been agonizing over a decision or difficult situation for quite some time. Then he mentions it, only to receive a quick, "Why don't you . . . ?" That actually communicates, "You're stupid. This is no problem at all. It's solvable in a matter of seconds."

The person who tends to relate as an advice-giver is also defining the relationship, as described in the opening chapter of this book. He is saying, "I'm up here and have the answer. You're down there and need to follow my advice."

Proverbs 15:23 says, "Everyone enjoys giving good advice." But the 28th verse of that same chapter says, "A good man thinks before he speaks."

The Patron
A variation on the ready advice theme is played when someone says very quickly, "I know *just* how you feel." Or in talking to a younger person, someone may say, "I felt just like that when I was your age."

These statements are meant to be supportive, but they usually backfire, because they communicate, "I can see right through you. It's very simple. Everyone has this problem; it's no big deal. All you need to do is. . . ."

This ready "support" often makes the other person feel silly, or petty, or small in your eyes; and yet he has felt he had a very deep problem. Of course, he may simply conclude you just don't understand, which may well be correct.

Unless we listen, we will not create an environment where a relationship can be developed or where truth can be heard. And the reactions we have been describing do not constitute true listening.

The Judge

Another block to listening is the habit of judging what another person says. Instead of really listening to the person or what he's saying, one is making value judgments about whether the person has done the right or the smart thing. This does not create an environment where true communication can take place, and where a person feels that he is being heard.

Don't misunderstand. There are times when very hard-nosed confrontations need to occur. But we must overcome what seems an almost built-in reflex to make value judgments about people all the time they are talking. This prevents our doing any kind of constructive listening.

The Teacher

Another hindrance to listening is the tendency we have to be in a hurry to teach a lesson. A child may relate something to the parent, and the parent has these wheels turning in the back of his head. He is thinking, *What generalization, what principle can my child learn from this.* And he quits listening to the child.

Consider the automatic reflex of a mother or a father when a child comes in and says, "Mommy, Johnny hit me!"

"Well, what did *you* do to make him hit you?"

They are looking for some principle to teach the child, rather than listening, and recognizing the child's feelings, and dealing with those feelings.

There is a place for teaching, of course. But everything a child does or says should not be the occasion for a lecture. One daughter said of her mother, "She doesn't talk, and she never listens; she just preaches."

The most common complaint of adolescence is, "My parents never listen to me. Every time I say something, I get sermon number 109. They never hear me." Of course, that's an exaggeration. It's not *never*, but that's the feeling young people too often get.

The Disciplined Listener

Real listening creates an atmosphere of acceptance that will make the person better able to hear and respond to any truth you may wish to communicate.

But good listening takes practice; it's actually a discipline. It doesn't come easily or naturally. It is a great ability to bring to the service of Christ and the help of people. It requires us to "tune in" the other person. It's a mental step of becoming really aware of *them*, instead of ourselves only.

Sometimes you can see somebody, but you don't really see him. It's amazing how we can tune people and situations out. Once I was driving down the highway when this happened. I was seeing, but not seeing. Suddenly I realized that the car in front of me had stopped; and my adrenal glands turned inside out as I hit the brakes.

We must develop the discipline of seeing and hearing the other person. It's a Christian responsibility: "Let every man be *swift to hear,* slow to speak, slow to wrath" (James 1:19, KJV).

Try it. Say to yourself, *I'm really going to tune him in today.* You may not make it more than 30 minutes through your daily routine before you will already be tuning people out. Listening doesn't come naturally; it has to be developed.

Dick was a hard-driving businessman who did learn to listen to his wife. Dick had a tremendous desire to be successful . . . and nagging fears of failure which he compensated for by working very hard and by doing many things that brought him before the public. He also had a powerful drive to acquire material goods that would give him the appearance of being successful.

His wife, in the meantime, was feeling increasingly left out. She also felt that he was going on some sort of ego trip and therefore took it upon herself to puncture his ego balloon whenever possible.

He responded to this by further withdrawing from her and increasing his activities outside the home. When he finally realized that much of her negativity was in fact a plea for more emotional involvement between them, he began to listen to her more carefully.

As he did so, he was able to understand some of her fears and needs, talk with her openly, and be more affectionate. Her entire attitude changed dramatically. She became supportive instead of opposing, sympathetic instead of critical.

To build a close relationship, practice the following communication exercise, which especially includes listening:

1. Allow time each day to talk, to share feelings and ideas, especially avoiding the communication and listening blocks.

2. One person must talk while the other listens in silence.

3. The listener must express what he has heard the speaker say, without adding anything new or stating any of his own feelings or reactions.

4. The listener must express what the speaker *meant*. If the speaker does not agree that the listener has expressed exactly what was meant, the exercise must be repeated, though the speaker need not express himself in exactly the same terms the second time as he attempts to communicate his feelings or views.

5. When the speaker agrees that he has really been heard, and the listener has, to the speaker's satisfaction, spoken back what was meant, roles are reversed. The speaker becomes listener and the exercise is repeated.

If we refuse to learn to listen, we should not deceive ourselves by trying to tell people anything.

The Bible says we must speak the truth in love (Eph. 4:15). And love, as we saw in chapter 6, is an attitude that may be taken by an act of the will and includes showing respect, faith, hope, endurance, patience, and kindness toward someone. This certainly includes listening. We must develop this loving attitude, without which our words are likely to fall on deaf ears.

Relate as God Commands

The wives of physicians and preachers or other people who are involved in performing services to others, often have a double whammy laid on them. The husband is highly committed to his work, puts in long hours, has talked to people all day, and when he comes home wants "peace and quiet." The wife may feel angry and resentful over his relative abandonment of her. At the same time she feels guilty because he is working so hard and is helping people. Therefore the anger is often pushed down only to have it seep out in anxiety, depression, or finally, angry, explosive reactions.

Regardless of any man's position, no matter how important or needed or helpful his work, if he does not help his wife feel that she is first in his life, he is not loving her as Christ loved the Church. He is not fulfilling his responsibility at home as Ephesians 5:25 commands.

Of course, if the wife were more attentive to his needs and less focused on her own, she might make more effort to guard his peace and quiet, particularly when he first gets home, without making demands on him. He then might be more willing to be available.

A physician who kept unreasonably long hours asked me one time, "Why should I come home where I'm treated like a peasant, when I'm treated like a king at work?"

It is possible for a person to interrupt these self-perpetuating cycles by beginning to relate to others as unto the Lord. By God's grace, one can break out of the pattern of simply being a reactor, of fighting for one's rights, of defending oneself. The person who calls upon God for strength to respond as Scripture commands can bring healing to his relationships.

Donna was an extremely insecure young woman who had grave fears that she would fail as a wife and mother. She often was one step short of folding up or going to pieces. She was constantly frustrated and disappointed in her husband, Hal, because he did not allay her fears by stating in detail what his plans were.

She felt threatened by his easygoing attitude and berated him as being irresponsible. He reacted with more withdrawal, to which she reacted with tantrums or by producing crises designed to draw him into her life more. This had the effect of pushing him even further away.

Finally, as part of his Christian commitment, Hal began to assert leadership in the home. Donna rebelled at first, but, as he demonstrated more and more the love that should go with leadership, she gained a sense of security and began to relax. He was then more willing to spend time with her and let her share her feelings, which brought them closer together.

Their self-perpetuating destructive cycle was interrupted by both positioning themselves under God in the role which He designed for them, and doing it in love.

That is, she began to allow him to be the head of the house, showing honor and respect for him, rather than trying to force him into some image she felt would bring her greater security. He, on the other hand, began to take responsible leadership, not in a dictatorial or autocratic way, but in a way that communicated understanding. He felt strong and respected. She felt secure and loved.

It was meant to be that way.

11

"We Must Pray for Betsy"

I described in chapter 1 how my wife, Betsy, as a teenager, tended to play the role of the ding-a-ling in order to gain acceptance. Those around her reacted as if the clown or the scatterbrain were the real person.

Today Betsy is anything but the ding-a-ling or scatterbrain. She is warm, honest, sensitive, perceptive, and a person with whom others feel comfortable.

One of the highest compliments Betsy has paid me is that I have affirmed her as a person. I took her seriously, and knew there was much more to her than the scatterbrained cheerleader who put the referee's penalty flag in her pocket.

She has said that I would laugh as much as anyone else when she said something funny. I seemed interested in her comments and thoughts, whatever the subject. Other people had laughed at her silliness, and she would capture some attention and get satisfaction from doing kooky things. I didn't laugh if she did silly things or put herself down in some way

Betsy said, "Eventually I learned I didn't have to do kooky things to get attention." More important, she felt loved, respected, and needed. Husbands and wives could avoid many unnecessary battles and ensure a growing relationship if they would show each other more positive appreciation, kindness, and consideration.

It is particularly important that parents give positive affirmation to their children. Many young people have told me that the only time they get any attention is when they are doing something wrong. We need to give them recognition and praise when they do well. Furthermore, when they act from good motives, we should praise them even if the performance is not always that outstanding. How many children have been disillusioned and discouraged because even when they try to do something good, they are criticized for it!

A Sense of Wonder

Joyce Landorf, writing in *Power for Living*, gives a good example of positive affirmation of children:

"One of the most precious things my mother developed in me was the sense of wonder.

"I guess all children are born with a sense of wonder, but to reach adulthood with it intact and fully matured is practically a miracle.

"I was only a second- or third-grader when I first noticed a field of yellow dandelions while on my way home from school one day. I waded into that glorious golden sea of sunshine, picked all the blossoms my hands could hold, and ran all the way home. I flung the door open wide and shouted, 'Here, Mother, *these are for you!*'

"At that moment, my mother was engaged in a Bible study with a roomful of ladies from our church. She had two options: shush me up, or develop my sense of wonder.

"In slow magnificent awe she laid her books on the table, knelt beside me, and took my gift.

"'Oh, they are beautiful, beautiful, beautiful,' she said over and over again. (She *could* have told me they were messy weeds.) 'I love them because you gave them to me.' (She *could* have given me a lecture on picking flowers on private property.) 'I'm going to set them on our table for our centerpiece tonight.' (She *could* have told me they'd never last the afternoon and aside from drooping would make my father sneeze.)"

Affirming those around us, whether children or adults, is one of the most powerful ways of influencing them in a helpful way. Jesus showed great affirmation toward His disciples, who often were petty, vindictive, and simply unaware of who Jesus was and what He came to do. True, He confronted them with their faults, but He also affirmed to them that they were of tremendous value to God the Father and to Him. And He committed Himself and His Father to love them, promised that He would never forsake them, and that no man could ever take them from His care, love, and comfort. When Peter had the insight that Jesus was the Christ, the anointed One, the Messiah, He said, "Blessed art thou, Simon . . ." (Matt. 16:17, KJV).

Ephesians 6:4 emphasizes this positive approach. "Now a word to you parents. Don't keep on scolding and nagging your children, making them angry and resentful. Rather, bring them up with the loving discipline the Lord Himself approves, with suggestions and godly advice." Colossians 3:21 says, "Fathers, don't scold your children so much that they become discouraged and quit trying."

The Family of God

One of our privileges and responsibilities as members of the family of God (the body of Christ) is to support one another. There are tremendous promises in Scripture concerning Christians who will come together as the body of Christ in honesty, openness, warmth, love, prayer, and action. People have a powerful need for this sharing relationship, and if it is not afforded within the confines of a particular church, it will be sought elsewhere.

If the body of Christ is truly going to function as it was designed, its members are going to have to become more honest and open than the average Christian is willing to be. I believe all Christians sooner or later come to a crossroads of tremendous importance.

When a person makes his initial commitment to Christ, he often experiences a sense of release. His guilt is gone. He is free and no longer bowed down with sin, alienation, and self-centeredness. A new concept of himself as a child of God and of life's purpose begins to dawn on him. It's a great experience.

Sooner or later, however, the Christian realizes he is not always confident, he is not always victorious, and sometimes he has a spirit of fear, not of love and of power and of a sound mind (see 2 Tim. 1:7). He can't seem to "do all things" through Jesus Christ (see Phil. 4:13).

The Christian at this point begins to make some very important decisions and take some crucial actions. One route he may take leads to Christian neuroticism; the other leads to growth, maturity, and fulfillment, though not without pain.

When the Christian faces the fact that his new life is not one long, unbroken, joyous succession

of blessings, he may have all kinds of emotional reactions that are antichristian. There will be times
when he is lustful, when he is petty, jealous, hostile, proud. He will experience anxiety, depression,
doubt.

At this point, one either faces and admits his continuing need for help from the Lord and through
fellow Christians, or he comes to the conclusion he
must pretend these undesirable feelings and doubts
aren't there. If he takes the latter course, his Christian life will subsequently be characterized by
faking it instead *of making it.*

To the degree one is influenced by teaching or
preaching that implies that Christians don't have
these feelings, thoughts, and reactions, he is in extreme danger of taking the fake-it route. This is
one of the twists that can be given to Christianity
that converts it into a mechanism to deny reality
and to go on a mask-wearing, self-righteous trip.
The fact is we are still human, and we still have
the egocentric child kicking and screaming inside.
It is true we have the new nature of Christ within,
but there is still conflict. The seventh chapter of
Romans describes this type of conflict.

Many Christians deny their real condition and
try to present the image that everything is always
joyous. They sometimes find fellow mask-wearing
Christians to support them in their neurotic stand.
This may work for a while, but shortly things start
eating away. Feelings are bottled up inside, and
they will come out in anxiety or depression or psychosomatic disorders.

Negative feelings that are bottled up have destructive effects, and there are many Christians who
suffer from this because they believe a Christian
must pretend no negative feelings are there. Such

Christians wear their masks, play their games, but don't really know each other. As a result, they don't have the kind of sharing that the Scriptures say we should.

James 5:16 says, "Admit your faults to one another and pray for each other so that you may be healed. The earnest prayer of a righteous man has great power and wonderful results."

Galatians 6:1-3 says, "Dear brothers, if a Christian is overcome by some sin, you who are godly should gently and humbly help him back on to the right path, remembering that next time it might be one of you who is in the wrong. Share each other's troubles and problems and so obey our Lord's command. If anyone thinks he is too great to stoop to this, he is fooling himself; he is really a nobody."

Other Scriptures quoted in chapter 3 also talk about the importance of Christians coming together honestly and openly, sharing, supporting, and confronting each other in a loving way, and praying for each other. This is a great experience, but one that many Christians miss because they or others they know refuse to take the risk of open, honest sharing.

Why Pretend?

One time in a Sunday School class on love within the family, Betsy admitted she sometimes had hateful feelings toward me or the children. The other members of the class clearly were not used to such honesty and immediately hid behind a pious cloak, suggesting they should pray for poor Betsy, who obviously was in dire straits as a Christian.

Many are afraid to take the type of risk Betsy took because others might think they are not very good Christians if they admit some of the foolish things they do and the destructive thoughts and feelings they have.

Betsy's honesty in the class ultimately paid off, however, and others began to share some of their problems. They began to function as the body of Christ should function. They could pray honestly and specifically for each other.

The pretense and the cover-up attitude exhibited by many Christians seems so ironic and unnecessary. After all, we come to Christ in the first place by honestly recognizing that we can't make it on our own, we're off-center, we're rebels, and that we want Him to clean up our lives, enter into our lives and be our Lord. Why do so many Christians have trouble retaining this kind of honest confession as an ongoing life style?

I believe it is to correct this type of error that the Apostle John wrote to *Christians*, "If we walk in the light as He is in the light, we have fellowship one with another and the blood of Jesus Christ His Son cleanseth us from all sin. If we say that we have no sin we deceive ourselves and the truth is not in us. If we confess our sins, He is faithful and just to forgive us our sins and to cleanse us from all unrighteousness" (1 John 1:7-9, KJV).

The person who practices the concept of walking in the light, is able to maintain an openness and honesty before the Lord and before fellow Christians. Thus he is constantly receiving cleansing and healing, and having fellowship.

Gifts

One of the important truths about the body of Christ is that individual members have different gifts, different needs, and different contributions to make. We have some gifts by birth (creation).

Others are acquired, and still others are given in a special way by the Holy Spirit. We have talked about our identity by creation, by redemption, and (in the body of Christ) by corporation.

Through all this, we should realize how extremely important we are. The habit many people have of putting themselves down is actually sin. We are each one a part of God's masterpiece, His workmanship, after we have been redeemed (Eph. 2: 10).

As we recognize who we are and what our unique gifts are, and as we allow the Holy Spirit to work through us, we begin to function as we were designed. I want to reemphasize the *diversity* of the gifts, because so many Christians are critical and divisive, trying to force others into being like themselves.

The Bible says, "God has given each of us the ability to do certain things well. So if God has given you the ability to prophesy, then prophesy whenever you can—as often as your faith is strong enough to receive a message from God. If your gift is that of serving others, serve them well. If you are a teacher, do a good job of teaching. If you are a preacher, see to it that your sermons are strong and helpful. If God has given you money, be generous in helping others with it. If God has given you administrative ability and put you in charge of the work of others, take the responsibility seriously. Those who offer comfort to the sorrowing should do so with Christian cheer " (Rom. 12:6-8).

"To one person the Spirit gives the ability to give wise advice; someone else may be especially good at studying and teaching, and this is his gift from the same Spirit. He gives special faith to another, and to someone else the power to heal the sick. He gives power for doing miracles to some, and to others power to prophesy and preach. He gives someone else the power to know whether evil spirits are speaking through those who claim to be giving God's messages—or whether it is really the Spirit of God who is speaking. [That is, some people seem to have the gift of discerning whether someone has gotten off on the wrong track, is under the influence of a false spirit, or is giving false messages.] Still another person is able to speak in languages he never learned; and others, who do not know the language either, are given power to understand what he is saying. It is the *same and only* Holy Spirit who gives all these gifts and powers, deciding *which* each one of us should have" (1 Cor. 12: 8-11).

Paul admonished Timothy to be sure to use the abilities God had given him. "Throw yourself into your tasks so that everyone may notice your improvement and progress" (1 Tim. 4:15).

One important fact to remember about all these gifts is that they are *gifts*. Their source is in God, not us. So they are never a basis for pride. "What are you so puffed up about?" Paul asked the gifted Christians at Corinth. "What do you have that God hasn't given you? And if all you have is from God, why act as though you are so great, and as though you have accomplished something on your own?" (1 Cor. 4:7)

Another important fact to remember is that all our gifts are given us for the purpose of enabling us to help others. They are not for our prestige or self-congratulation or even primarily for our own spiritual benefit. This is emphasized repeatedly in 1 Corinthians 14, where we read such expressions as, "Since you are so anxious to have special gifts from the Holy Spirit, ask Him for the very best, for those that will be of *real help to the whole church*" (v. 12, see also vv. 4, 5, 6, 17, 19, 26).

No Grinding Service

Obviously these Scriptures and the whole concept of gifts—also assumes one will be a *part of a fellowship* of Christians. God does not intend you to live as a Christian in isolation from other Christians.

Why am I emphasizing this subject of gifts? Because I think one of the most powerful liberating forces many Christians could find would be to recognize their unique place within the body of Christ and to utilize the gifts they have. When a person begins to work this way, his service is not such a grinding struggle.

When you see people in the church whose tongues are hanging out, knocking themselves out doing all kinds of things, and about to have a breakdown because of it, I can guarantee you they are not following the Holy Spirit. They are usually letting other people dictate to them what they should be doing. They're so concerned about what somebody else is going to think that they let themselves be talked into doing all kinds of things that may not be in accord with their gifts at all. They do these things lest someone say or think that they are not good Christians.

God has made us the way we are for a purpose, and it is really important for us to be aware of our gifts. In fact, this is one of the responsibilities of the body of Christ. We ought to be sharing with each other in such a way that we discover our gifts, and use them. If we really want to reach fulfillment and grow, we've got to put these gifts into action. Some Christians are so busy with spiritual one-upmanship games they are unable to relax in the Lord and allow the Holy Spirit to use them in their uniqueness. They seem driven to model themselves after someone else or to force others to behave as they do.

Someone else may think that you ought to sing in the choir or serve on the social concerns committee, but that may not be right for you. You must learn to say, "No, that's not for me." Let them know that you're going with the gifts God has given you. This is how growth takes place. Many very fatigued Christians are victims of this tendency to do all kinds of things they weren't intended to do. They get caught up in the Christian rat race! They are going against the grain, and it's such a struggle.

Another related neurotic notion is: "I'm the *right arm* of God; I've got to be all things to everybody." You can go crazy doing this. There is so much suffering in the world; there are so many good things that you could be doing. You could easily spread yourself so thin that you're nothing but a bundle of nerves, frustrated, doing nothing particularly well, and feeling guilty about the whole mess.

That syndrome is so unnecessary. The body of Christ is composed of *all* of the parts. The Apostle Paul emphasizes this over and over again (see 1 Cor. 12). The arm needs to behave like an arm, not try to be the whole body. And a leg needs to be a leg. Maybe there are some people who can walk on their hands, but even if they are skilled in doing it, it gets very tiresome, and they can't hold out for long. That isn't the way the hands were designed. Yet many Christians who are hands, let us say, are trying to behave like feet.

So it is really important for a Christian to be aware of his gifts and then to do something about them. A Christian needs to develop this concept: *I have a sphere of influence, and I have certain gifts God has given me. I belong to a group of fellow Christians, the body of Christ. As part of the body, I have a unique contribution. I also uniquely receive from all the members. All together, we are able to help one another as well as to reach out to others in the most fulfilling and effective way.*

Part V

*How Can We
Untwist Our Lives?*

12

"I Don't Smoke;
I Just Flare Up"

One Sunday we were going through the usual has-
sle of getting four children and ourselves ready
for Sunday School. Our youngest son, John, who
was five years of age at the time, was operating
exclusively in extra slow motion. After 30 minutes
of doing I don't know what, he was still in his pa-
jamas and had yet to put on the first stitch of
clothes.

Betsy began giving him the hurry-up treatment.
He finally found his underwear somewhere, but he
didn't have any socks. This seemed to jam his computer, so he sat down, apparently hoping the socks
would miraculously appear. After due investigative
research, Betsy made a determination that the missing socks were in our older son's room downstairs,
and she said, with some irritation, "Go on to Jim's
room and get your socks, and hurry up."

John dutifully went downstairs to the door of his
brother's room to get his socks. His big brother,
Jim, stood in the doorway saying, "You can't come
into my room!" (John had the habit of helping himself to Jim's paper and pencils.) So John was stand-

ing in front of the door, tears streaming down his cheeks—caught between the anger of mother upstairs and the formidable opposition of big brother downstairs.

I was downstairs and caught the full impact of John's frustration as he stood there in the hallway outside Jim's door. When Jim closed the door in his brother's tearful face, I charged down the hall. Even as I was doing so, a split-second, fleeting thought went through my head. *No, you are giving in to this rage—you're blowing it.*

I could have had restraint at that point, but I didn't. Instead, I threw open the door and pushed Jim onto his bed. He cowered there, scared to death of his huge, angry father as I stood over him, shook my fist in his face, and demanded, "Why don't you have a little patience and kindness?"

Then we all went to Sunday School and church. It took 12 hours for me to get straightened out inside and then to go to Jim and make things right with him. I began by talking about how he probably felt when I descended on him, and also how John probably felt when he was on the receiving end of Jim's unreasonableness. And so we were able to get back together.

I want to give some clear specifics on *how* to bring healing into one's life and relationships. I am giving anger special consideration, because the pattern for dealing with that painful emotion is a model for dealing with almost any communication block or any hurt that occurs in our relationships. Another reason for emphasizing anger is that Christians are often unwilling or unable to face their own angry reactions and deal with them constructively.

The Need for Restraint

Now, I am not suggesting that when the confrontation between Jim and John took place I should have been syrupy and kind and said, "Now, Jim, don't behave like that." Nor that I should have pretended that no anger was within me. No, I should have dealt with my anger honestly and openly *but nondestructively,* as I will detail later. In that instance, I was dealing with anger destructively.

As a result, nothing beneficial was taking place. Jim was learning only that he had a fearsome father.

When we overreact, when we don't show restraint, especially in discipline, or in dealing with another person, all the person sees is our unreasonableness. He doesn't see what role he played in the problem. A person naturally wants to avoid looking at his mistakes. So if someone else overreacts or otherwise gives the person an excuse to divert his attention, he will do so. This is the error of the parent who habitually comes on too strong. It is an "international crisis" if there is a track on the floor somewhere, or it is going to be the "destruction of the universe" if the child spills his milk. Children don't learn from these reactions. All they hear is an unreasonable, angry, fearsome parent. And they usually learn how to tune the parent out.

This points up the first important principle for dealing with anger. We must use restraint. Flying into a rage leads to evil. "He that is soon angry dealeth foolishly," says Proverbs 14:17 (KJV). "He that is slow to anger is better than the mighty; and he that ruleth his spirit than he that taketh a city" (Prov. 16:32, KJV).

Now, all I have said about restraining anger

can be readily accepted by most people, especially by Christians. Having said that, many Christians think there is little more to say. The fact is, we have hardly begun, because dealing with anger constructively involves much more than restraint. Restraint alone, in the long run, leads to more trouble and causes more problems than it solves.

Many Christians simply will not recognize that they have problems with anger. It is hidden behind "righteous indignation." I believe that in many ways anger is a greater problem with Christians than it is with others. How many Elks Clubs have split over whether to have a kitchen or not, as some churches have? When was the last time that a president of a Kiwanis Club was asked to resign because his wife's skirts were too short, as has been the case with some pastors? Of course, some churches are filled with people who are not Christians, who certainly add to the turmoil, but true Christians have many problems with anger also.

Recognizing Anger

It is painful to recognize and admit that we have problems with anger, Christians particularly feel guilty about anger, so they substitute other words for it in an attempt to evade the issue. Rather than admitting we are angry, we say we are *hurt*. Or if you're from some sections of the South, someone's aggravating behavior may make you *ill*. Others are *disappointed*, or *frustrated*, or a little *disturbed*, or slightly *out of sorts*. All of these words are used to describe, or to disguise, a reaction varying in intensity from a desire to assault someone with words to the urge to use a club on them.

There is a great need for people to be honest with themselves and to recognize anger. This is the first step toward resolving "anger sickness" in its many forms. There's no hope of healing if we don't even recognize our anger.

Anger Goes Underground

Many people are very aware of being angry, but they are unable to deal with it. They are intimidated and threatened by it. "Oh, I shouldn't get angry," they say. So they push it down inside. In many respects, this is one of the most destructive ways of dealing with anger, and consciously or unconsciously, it is one of the most common "Christian" methods of dealing with anger. Really, the anger is not *dealt with* at all. It is pushed down, denied.

When anger goes underground, it introduces one into a vicious cycle. So many negative emotional charges accumulate within that one becomes like a volcano inside. The anger rumbling around in there bubbles up from time to time, which is very threatening to the person. He is also very vulnerable to any new anger or new frustration, because he is already carrying a near capacity load of anger, and is afraid of it.

Now even less capable of dealing with additional anger that comes, he quickly pushes that down and adds it to the bubbling cauldron. When this pattern develops, some sort of eruption is certain to occur. However, the eruption is not necessarily recognized as anger. It may assume some other form. This prevents him from taking proper corrective action.

As has already been mentioned, when hurtful, negative feelings are pushed down inside, they will come out one way or another. Either they will show in a certain type behavior, or in distressful symptoms such as anxiety or depression, or in psychosomatic problems such as headaches, high blood pressure, or stomach trouble.

Here are some specific ways unresolved anger may influence our behavior.

Overcompensation

One reaction, to use a psychoanalytic term, is counterphobic. This means displaying an opposite reaction. The extreme counterphobic who is afraid of heights jumps out of airplanes, sky dives. The counterphobic who is angry may be very solicitous and kind.

Sometimes those who ooze sweetness from every pore are extremely angry people. Charles Dickens' character, Uriah Heep, is a good example of this. With every breath and action such people are protesting how much they care, how much love they have. And they knock themselves out attempting to prove it. Sometimes, just being around such a person makes one feel uncomfortable. Part of the discomfort comes from the sense that one is not dealing with the real person.

Helen was so sweet it was unreal. She was very compliant and quite concerned lest she hurt someone's feelings. She wore a continuous smile and everything was always all right. But to the utter amazement of her friends, and without any warning, she one day took her life. Suicide is one of the most angry acts a person can commit.

Janet was a young married woman who also came across as very sweet and very kind. She had a great deal of trouble recognizing when she was angry. She did realize that she was "sensitive" and easily hurt.

One of the symptoms that brought Janet into

therapy was a sudden overwhelming fear that she was going to hurt someone or lose control of herself in some way. She was also depression prone.

Janet found healing through recognizing and acknowledging her angry reactions to her husband, children, in-laws, and others. She could then deal with her anger appropriately instead of pushing it down. She could pray much more specifically and honestly, and this relieved her stored up hostility. This, in turn, enabled her to be more assertive and open with people. She was also more fun to be with because she was not so tense about the possibility of offending somebody.

Passive Hostility
Anger that is not dealt with may also be expressed in a passively hostile way. The person who is chronically late, who drags his feet, who is an obstructionist at business meetings, bringing up all sorts of trivia, very likely has problems in dealing with anger directly.

The husband who can't remember those things his wife asked him to pick up may well be clobbering her with his inability to remember things. Simply refusing to talk with someone or refusing to perform an act of kindness that would have been appreciated represents passive hostility.

Irritability
Many people who are unable to deal with anger at the real gut level have it spill out over inconsequential matters, and are generally irritable. Various mannerisms and habits those around them have—things which really aren't that important—set them off because there is so much anger stored within them already.

It's amazing the emotional charges that can get attached to trivial matters. The bathtub is not washed out after use, or a light is left burning, or part of the newspaper is misplaced, and this provokes an intense reaction. The person in this state seems to have a special built-in radar to pick up the slightest thing that is out of order. This is a miserable state to be in, but generalized irritability is often the price people pay for not dealing with the more basic issues that involve anger.

The Last Straw

Some of the most dramatic reactions to stored up anger occur when people finally erupt over "the last straw." They end up doing or saying something very foolish. Then what? They say, "I *knew* it didn't pay to get angry." And so they go right back underground with any recurring anger until the next volcanic eruption.

Brenda was an intelligent, sensitive woman who counseled others with their problems. She had a rather level-headed husband who was somewhat distant and a mother-in-law who was "impossible."

Brenda was unable to discuss many things with her husband at an intimate level, because he tended to withdraw. She became increasingly frustrated over little things her mother-in-law did as well as over little inconsiderate actions of her husband.

Finally, she had collected so many of these resentments that she was about to explode. Her husband went out of town on a bona fide business trip, leaving her up in the air concerning various matters he would not sit down and discuss with her. This was the last straw. While he was gone, she totally destroyed his hi-fi collection. When he got home, in order to maintain the offensive, she called him virtually every name in the book, which further reinforced his belief that she was unreasonable, and made it easier for him to ignore her legitimate complaints.

After it was all over, Brenda was chagrined and penitent and felt childish. She would have gone underground again with her feelings until the next volcanic eruption if it had not been for therapy which brought both her and her husband out into more open communication.

Anger-Induced Distress

Bottled up anger may come out disguised behind painful emotional symptoms such as anxiety, depression, tension. The person cannot figure out why he has these feelings. There seems to be no rhyme or reason for them. But he is tense and anxious most of the time, a victim of "free-floating anxiety."

Sometimes a person believes he knows why he is anxious, but whether he thinks he knows or not, often the underlying problem is anger.

Of course, anger is not the only source of depression but it is a common one. It is as if the person, not able to deal with anger, turns it in upon himself.

Sometimes the self-accusations that a depressed person typically makes are, in fact, feelings he or she has toward meaningful others (people we need and who need us). A person may say, "I wish I were dead." If you could get to the real gut-level of that, you might uncover some very murderous feelings toward meaningful others. But denying that such anger exists, the depressed person has really turned it inward.

It is ironic that so many people who are pushing anger down are acting from good motives. They want to be kind; they want to be nice; they don't want to cause disharmony. But they usually end up causing more disharmony than if they had dealt with their anger more openly. Certainly the person who is frequently tense or depressed cannot deal as lovingly and as effectively with others as a well-adjusted, happy person could.

Psychosomatic Illness

Repressed anger may come out in physical, psychosomatic symptoms: headaches, blood pressure problems, stomach troubles, and mysterious pains. Anger is not just a state of mind. It *chemically* influences the body.

Anger is a psychological and physiological reaction in the body, decreasing the blood supply to the stomach and increasing the blood supply to the muscles. The capacity to burn sugar is increased, eyes dilate, the muscle tone increases even to the point of quivering. All this energy and tension, if not dissipated, works destructively in our bodies.

Doris was a 40-year-old woman who was very angry, but extremely blocked in being able to express her anger, or *any* feelings for that matter. She was a Christian. She was also very aware of and critical about the fact that people don't behave the way they should. Doris had great difficulty in forming close relationships with people and felt uncomfortable around them. She was never able to develop a sense of being a part of the body of Christ in the framework of a local church.

Problems of anger, loneliness, depression could not be discussed with her. She seemed to feel that a Christian should not be depressed, and denied this was a problem for her.

All of these negative feelings began to come out

in physical symptoms. Doris felt physically exhausted and began to focus more and more on her body, which was beginning to produce a great deal of distress through various symptoms. She began to spend more time in bed. Her unresolved and unadmitted feelings actually were making Doris a chronic invalid.

The Overreactor

Problems with anger include more than just pushing it down. There are people who pour out their feelings at every opportunity and over the slightest provocation. Sometimes they are the proud graduates of psychiatric or group treatment. They say, "I'm free; I'm now a lion and no longer a mouse." While many people do need to be freed from being overinhibited and from pushing anger down, one can go to extremes in the other direction. Again, any truth can be given a slight twist that makes it destructive.

People who overreact to anger don't get ulcers. They *give* them! Such people are proud of the fact that they say what they think and what they feel, but they cause a great deal of hurt to others.

There's an old adage that the angriest person in the world is really the most frightened person in the world. I think there is a very powerful truth to that. Often the person who gives vent freely to anger is basically a very insecure, very frightened person. He assumes he's not going to be accepted, and he follows that antigolden rule principle, "Do unto others before they have a chance to do unto you."

Such a person assumes rejection. Insecure, on guard, he is keenly attuned to real or imagined negative statements, to verbal and nonverbal slights, and he's ready to let the other guy have it before the other guy has a chance to let him have it. This type of person is often very uncomfortable with tenderness or closeness. He fears he may be used, abused, tricked, and so he's always ready to come on strong. He is not dealing with anger constructively and is unlikely to build the type of relationships he needs to be a fulfilled person.

Sources of Anger

Why do we get angry in the first place? I have already suggested that the most basic emotion behind anger is *fear*. Real or assumed or anticipated rejection is certainly one of the most common causes of anger. It may be that we are ignored That's a type of rejection. People don't pay as much attention to us as we would like. They don't appreciate us as much as they should. Or we are the recipients of something that is more hostile. We are insulted, put down.

One of the reasons tension often fills the air over a discussion of religion or politics is that these are areas in which we feel very strongly. If these beliefs are challenged in some way, we feel threatened because they are a part of our very being. This means that if *our views* are disallowed, *we* are being rejected.

Some Christian "witnessing," is, in fact, a hostile attack on others. The Christian is threatened if others do not believe as he does. He becomes angry at the other person's lack of belief, and he attacks.

I got caught up in this one time in a conversation at a Christian Medical Society meeting. Two visiting freshmen began to reel off a lot of the statements that you will hear sometimes about

Christianity being myth and about how man has learned all these new things that pretty well explode the outmoded concepts of the Bible. My reaction to these men was not exactly compassionate. They were coming across as confident in their "new" knowledge that was supposed to show us Christians we were all wrong.

My ego response was, *Who do these two think they are? I worked through all that intellectual ego trip years ago. I know better than that. They act as if they've got something new to tell me.* My ego was being threatened; they were implying I was not as smart as they. So I began to put them down, to point out that their line of thinking wasn't all that logical.

I had a flash of insight in the midst of this encounter that I was winning this battle but losing these two young men. It was an agonizing thing to realize that my witness was really an expression of my hostility. I was rejecting these fellows and puffing up my own ego.

I was able to tell them this later, and that drew them back some. But this is often our problem; we're fearful. Somebody's not going to agree with us. We're being ignored, attacked, rejected. I was demonstrating my vulnerability when these two men suggested Christianity was irrational . . . and by projection, that I was irrational.

Other people are vulnerable in other areas. They may fear that they are going to be abused or manipulated, and often feel, rightly or wrongly, that they have been.

The repetitive theme of one man at a marriage conference was that he had to be on guard in all of his relationships because everybody was trying to put one over on him in one way or another. He was an angry man, and his relationship with his wife was not close. He was too busy protecting himself from real or imagined threats to do much reaching out to others.

Faulty Expectations

Another factor that predisposes us to anger is our faulty expectations. One reason it is not always constructive to just "express your anger," which seems to be some people's kick, is that your reason for being angry may be wrong in the first place. You may have unreasonable expectations. You need to deal with your expectations instead of popping off angrily every time someone doesn't live up to them.

An example of this is the overly dependent person, who is looking for someone who will meet all of his emotional needs, which are excessive. He comes to husband, to wife, to friend, to pastor, to counselor and appears as a lump of clay: very cooperative and very compliant.

It is only a matter of time until the dependent person is disappointed. His needs are not being met the way he would like. He is angry but is afraid to express his anger because then he might be rejected and never receive help. So he keeps it inside, and gets depressed. This forces more care from the giving person.

I dealt with Max for two years. He had gone through a succession of pastors. His wife was ready to pull her hair out because of him. He would latch on to one person for a while, and then get disappointed and hurt.

Of course, what happens is that the person on the giving end at some point begins to realize that whatever he's doing is not enough. He gets frustrated and begins backing away. The other person reads this as rejection, and so now another giving person has disappointed him.

I tried to help Max realize that I knew he was angry at me, and it was all right. He had many needs, and I knew that I couldn't meet all these needs. It was OK for him to be disappointed, but he also had to realize that his expectations were great.

The day he realized that he could be angry with me and I would not reject him but would help him see how he might become more independent, he turned a corner. He began to get over his depression and to change his life-style that was self-defeating.

There is a corollary to this in the expectations that I observe very commonly between husbands and wives. It's based on the myth that if you're in love, and certainly if you're married, it makes your partner a mind reader.

Very commonly when I am seeing a couple in marriage counseling, I suggest they become more honest, more open, and more communicative in expressing their needs. Often the wife (or the husband) will say, in a reproachful tone, that the other person ought to know what the needs are. Then the patient expresses a psuedo-logic that if one tells what one's needs are the other person is not giving spontaneously.

A similar notion is sometimes expressed after one mate has begun to show volitional love. The other will say, "Yes, he (or she) showed me kindness, but only because you told him (her) to." As if that made it less acceptable!

This misconception of love traces back to the romantic notion that some Prince Charming will come along who will automatically understand all our needs and devote himself full-time to meeting them. The volitional love concept of 1 Corinthians 13 is not understood or accepted.

Volitional love involves a commítment to another person. The more open that person can be in revealing needs, the more specific and adequate can be the volitional lover's response. Many people will not express their needs, but, oh, how hurt they are when their needs are not met! They have this egocentric idea: everybody else should know what I need and should meet my need.

So whether we expect other people to be mind readers or simply have excessive expectations, we are prone to be angry as a result of our egocentricity.

Anger that arises from excessive expectations may drive a person into serious emotional illness. For example, Martin was quite sensitive to whether other people were being absolutely truthful or behaving exactly as he thought they should. When they did not, he was able to tell them about it rather forcefully. However, he tended to carry resentment and write people off as "no good" if they did not live up to his expectations.

He finally was carrying so many negative emotions inside that he began to imagine various people were against him. He became increasingly depressed and suspicious. He began to interpret all events as if they related to him in some harmful way. If a car happened to be behind him, they were following him to do some mischief to him. Anything that happened during the day that was a bother, or that obstructed him, and his work, was thought to be done on purpose in order to harrass him.

It took medication to help Martin begin to think more rationally and to clear up some of his depression. However, the final healing only could take place when he reaffirmed his commitment to Jesus Christ and began to seek forgiveness from those whom he had written off and toward whom he had been harboring resentment.

Anger takes many forms and has many sources. And it has many destructive effects. Yet anger itself is not always wrong, as we shall see in the next chapter. It all depends on how one deals with it.

13

Your Temper May Be Hazardous to Your Health

We should thank the Lord for our capacity to feel and be aware of anger. It is one of the most important warning signals that we can have of something wrong, of some situation that needs attention. Anger is by no means an evil in itself. It's one of the most important emotions we can have because of the motivation it gives to us. It's what we do with it that counts.

An often quoted—and often misunderstood—passage of Scripture is Matthew 5:22, 23 (Jesus speaking): "If you are only angry even in your own home, you are in danger of judgment. If you call your friend an idiot, you are in danger of being brought before the court. And if you curse him, you are in danger of the fires of hell."

When you are angry, you are so motivated to act, that you are in danger of handling it the wrong way. *Be angry, call someone an idiot, curse him*—each of these is a progressively angrier reaction, going the wrong direction.

But notice, Jesus is talking in terms of *danger*. Because anger motivates us to act, we are in danger

185

of going the wrong way. But we could deal with anger in a constructive way.

Dealing With Anger

We began the previous chapter by mentioning the need for restraint. Don't join the spew-it-all-out crowd. They may feel good about their release of tension, but they may also be very destructive. The Bible clearly says we should show restraint in our reactions.

Proverbs 14:17 basically teaches that if you have a short temper, chances are you're going to behave foolishly. This is also the message of Proverbs 14:29: "A wise man controls his temper. He knows that anger causes mistakes."

"Stop your anger! Turn off your wrath" (Ps. 37:8). "A wise man restrains his anger and overlooks insults. This is to his credit" (Prov. 19:11). "Don't be quick-tempered—that is being a fool" (Ecc. 7:9).

In other words, the Christian must express something other than mere stimulus-response. There needs to be a factor operating *between* stimulus and response, between input and output, if we are to deal with life constructively. This is in part the message of Philippians 2:5, "Let this mind be in you which was also in Christ Jesus" (KJV). If we have the Spirit of Christ operating within us, we will not be just *reactors;* we will bring something new, something healing into our relationships.

Very often, when we are reacting to anger, we have a split second in which we recognize what we are doing. If we would commit ourselves to Christ at that moment, we could avoid many mistakes. As I was charging across the room in reaction to Jim and his younger brother, as I described in the previous chapter, I had such a moment when I could have stopped. When we give in to feelings without allowing the mind of Christ to operate within us, we are behaving like an animal reacting to a stimulus.

Avenge Not

Other Scriptures dealing with anger warn against being vengeful. Some of the most unhappy people are those who are caught up in seeking revenge. You know the attitude: *I'll show him; I'm going to get him.* All our neurons are charged up. We have a third eye and ear just waiting to catch our enemy. This poisons us. A very familiar Scripture says, "Vengeance is mine, I will repay, saith the Lord" (Rom. 12:19, KJV).

Essentially this passage goes on to say much the same thing that Jesus taught: do good to those who persecute you. If your enemy is hungry, feed him; if he is thirsty, give him a drink. In so doing you "heap coals of fire on his head" (Rom. 12:20, KJV).

When we return kindness for evil, we are, in a sense, initiating a sacrificial redemptive action. Paul is talking about interrupting the vicious cycle of action and reaction, evil done and evil returned. This is how a Christian can be a creative actor rather than merely a reactor.

Now, there can be a neurotic kink or twist of this principle. Sometimes we are not really trying to reverse the cycle but we are being drippingly sweet to someone who has mistreated us in an attempt to make him feel guilty. If we are really going to interrupt the cycle, and follow the intent of Scripture, we need to consider how the other person is hurting, what his complaints are, what his needs are, and commit ourselves to understand and help. *That* is interrupting the cycle.

Turning the Other Cheek

Another Scripture relating to anger says, "Whosoever shall smite thee on thy right cheek, turn to him the other also" (Matt. 5:39, KJV). Jesus was not so much pleading for passivity here as He was admonishing us not to be reactors. An interesting aspect of this Scripture is the fact that the right cheek is specified. Since most people are right-handed, the only way they can slap someone on the right cheek is with the back of their hand. That is the classical insult or challenge—a backhanded slap on the face. Without making an issue of that, any slap on the face is a challenge.

The neurotic interpretation of that verse is to suggest one should repress any angry reaction, pretend this doesn't bother him, and just wear his Christian mask as if all were well. I think I hear Jesus saying something quite different here. As we shall see from other Scriptures, Jesus intended for the Christian to be actively, appropriately, constructively assertive in dealing with anger.

Here, Jesus is saying, "Don't be so quick to feel insulted. Don't be so vulnerable that you feel you have to respond to every challenge, intended or not." Some people have such fragile egos that the slightest thing is a challenge. An example of this may be observed in some young people who are really struggling for identity. A mother may innocently say, "Honey, it's time to go to bed," and it's just like a national crisis.

"You're always telling me what to do. I'm not a baby!"

Some people never seem to outgrow this. Everything is a slap in the face to them, and the only way they can defend their integrity is to pick up the gauntlet, draw the sword, attack or counter-attack. I hear Christ saying, "Don't have such a fragile ego. Turn the other cheek. Yes, even if it may have been a real insult."

Going the Second Mile

Another Scripture that shows how the Christian is to be a creative actor rather than a reactor is Matthew 5:41: "And whosoever shall compel thee to go a mile, go with him twain" (KJV). Picture this scene in first-century Jerusalem. A Roman soldier comes along and forces a Jewish resident to carry his pack. Roman law required that the Jew must carry it one mile. Many Jews had stakes one mile from their homes so they knew exactly when the required service was done. But here is a Jew who continues bearing the soldier's pack into the second mile. Now, who is in control? It's not the Roman soldier any more. That Jew going the second mile is the one who is operating from a position of strength now.

There is a very powerful principle in this. When we do something because we have been nagged or forced into it, it does not come through to the other person as a gift. And we feel we are operating from a position of weakness. We are being forced or badgered into doing something.

But the person who goes the second mile is giving a gift. He hasn't been nagged into it. He hasn't been required by "law," and he is operating from a position of strength. He doesn't have to get hung up in his fragile ego, feeling subjugated, used, or hen-pecked. And the person who is the recipient of such a "second-mile" gift realizes it came from the other person's free will. If we are to be creative actors and bring healing into relationships, we need to learn more and more ways to go the second mile.

Confrontation Without Condemnation

This leads us to the most powerful principle in all the Scriptures for dealing with anger. I refer to the principle of *confrontation without condemnation*. There are many examples of this in the Scriptures. Paul openly confronted Peter, who in a weak, hypocritical moment, would not eat with some Gentiles for fear of what his Jewish brethren would say. Paul laid it on him pretty straight (Gal. 2:11-14).

Jesus did the same thing with the disciples when they were haggling over who was going to be the greatest in the kingdom of God. He confronted them, but did not condemn them (Mark 9:33-35).

Jesus also gave us this model: if your brother has a grievance against you, do not even go through your regular forms of worship until you have gone to your brother and straightened things out (see Matt. 5:23, 24). That's confrontation. Some Christians will pray in this situation and actually use prayer as a neurotic mechanism. That is, instead of going to the person and doing something about the problem, they just pray to God to forgive them or to heal the situation.

A similar principle applies when your brother has wronged you. It is still right for you to go to the person and straighten matters out. If the other person won't hear you when you confront him, go to him with some other people (see Matt. 18:15-17). There is nothing passive about this approach to anger.

The Scripture says we should be angry and sin not. Do not let the sun set on your wrath (see Eph. 4:26). This is a commandment to get anger out in the open and deal with it. A person who simply pretends not to be angry, pushing it down inside does exactly what the Scripture says *not* to do. He does let the sun set on his wrath, and he does give a mighty foothold to the devil.

Frankness or Flattery

Proverbs 27:5 says, "Open rebuke is better than hidden love" In other words, it is best to bring feelings out in the open. Even a negative action such as rebuke is better than love that is hidden, because only when feelings are brought out into the open can healing take place.

One could also say that open rebuke is likely to bring about open love. That is, it has been many people's experience that when they have gotten anger out in the open and dealt with it, they were afterward able to love better. They may have been shaking, quivering, overreacting, as they expressed their anger. Nevertheless, they got it out in the open, and they dealt with the issue squarely. They might even have been frightened by the intensity of their anger because so much had been locked up for so long. But the experience was a liberating one that allowed them to express love in a depth unknown previously.

People who want to keep things peaceful and don't want to be hurtful and who therefore bottle up anger inside, actually restrict their own freedom and ability to love. They are sitting on so much anger that they use up a lot of emotional energy just to control it.

"In the end [in the long run], people appreciate

frankness more than flattery" (Prov. 28:23).

A couple came to see me with serious marital problems. I saw the husband first. Afterward, when his wife came into the room, he jumped out of his seat and almost bowed. He was so courteous and proper that I felt as if I should perhaps introduce him to his wife!

That little act was symbolic of a great deal of the problem in their relationship. He was so nice. He was so kind and considerate. He always opened the door, always handled her chair for her, always got up when she walked in, but he *did this with everybody*. His flattering style made his wife feel as if she were living with a stranger, and she highly resented it. It would have been much more meaningful if he had treated her as a real, feeling, sharing person—not that he should have neglected to show her courtesy; most men need to show their wives more courtesy than they do.

It is much more meaningful to receive a compliment from someone we know is honest, who would also be critical if he felt it, than from a flatterer. Such frankness implies the person respects you and trusts you enough to feel that he can be open.

Jesus said, "Rebuke your brother if he sins, and forgive him if he is sorry" (Luke 17:3, 4). Even if this process takes place seven times a day, and he seeks forgiveness, forgive him. Jesus was not delivering a treatise on score-keeping and on that eighth time, you really let him have it. He was saying that we need to be frank, honest, open, and forgiving. If rebuke is called for, deliver it. But be forgiving If the person seeks forgiveness, forgive him. We need this balance between honesty, openness, directness, frankness, on the one hand, and acceptance, affirmation, forgiveness on the other.

Anger is one of the most difficult emotions to handle. When we have learned to handle anger, we can use the same principles to improve communications and relationships, whatever the issues. Therefore, what we are saying in these two chapters on anger should be considered as suggestive of ways to deal with a wide range of other emotions also.

It should be apparent by now that Scripture makes a very strong case for honest, open confrontation. It makes an equally strong case, however, for us to be loving, caring, forgiving, and healing. We must bring these two principles together. Here's how:

1. Take Your Responsibility

We need to be honest with ourselves, tuned into our feelings, and willing to state them. But we should take personal responsibility for them. It is never correct to say, "You make me so angry." The reaction is all yours, and you must take responsibility for it.

As we take personal responsibility for our feelings, we should be honest enough to point out that this is a problem for us. Say, "These are my feelings. I'm vulnerable in this area. I get uptight quickly when somebody is putting me down, and I feel that is what you are doing. I react against that, and I begin to get angry."

2. Describe the Results

After expressing our anger and admitting we are sensitive in this area, we can point out that the situation distresses us. We don't like feeling angry; we don't like the way this separates us. It makes us feel like we want to fight or leave, but we don't want the relationship to be that way.

When a person is communicating along these lines, he is less likely to trigger defensiveness or counterattack in the other person.

We must also resist the tendency to interpret the other person's motives or to make statements about his basic self. At all costs we should avoid statements such as, "Oh, you are just trying to make me angry." Or, "You always try to hurt me." Or, "You are mean just like your mother, like your whole family; they never liked me, and you don't either."

3. Allow Reaction
Of course, after we state our feelings, the other person is going to respond. No matter how well we have taken responsibility for our own feelings and expressed a desire not to have a rift between us, the other person will still want to counter with his own feelings.

At this point, it is extremely important for us not to start getting defensive, or coming on stronger, or disallowing his feelings. He has as much right to express his feelings as we do ours. If both of us can reveal our feelings in the context of a basic commitment to bring healing into the relationship and to correct the frustrations, then the relationship will become more meaningful, not in spite of the anger but in one sense because of it.

4. Push for Reconciliation
"Do not merely desire peaceful relations with God, with your fellow man, and with yourself, but pursue, go after them" (1 Peter 3:11, AMP).

We should actively push for forgiveness and reconciliation. Sometimes we will ask a person to forgive us and he will say, "Oh, it's all right; it didn't bother me." Then we let it drop. I suspect that in most instances the person who says it didn't bother him has his own ego problem of pride to some degree and doesn't want to admit he was bothered or that he lost his cool. He needs the experience of forgiving, as much as the offender needs the experience of seeking forgiveness.

If someone asks us to forgive him, we should clearly and graciously do so. The person who is walking in the light, walking in the Spirit rather than in the flesh, will have a sensitivity which will enable him to learn from the interaction of openly expressing feelings. That is, he will understand better how the other person feels and what the other person's needs are, and he will commit himself to meet them. The person who is walking in the flesh simply wants to vindicate his point of view, force the other person into some downed position, twist the knife, and self-righteously fight for his cause.

While we were in the process of moving to Atlanta, Betsy was busy refinishing some furniture. I was out passing the football with the boys. Betsy wanted me to help her, and step by step we violated the principles I have been sharing with you in this book.

I resisted her request for help, pointing out that it was more important for me to play with the boys. My masculine ego was resisting being directed. Her response was straight from the feminine ego, which now felt rejected. She said something to make me feel guilty.

Rather than listening to her hurt and frustration, I counterattacked with a guilt-provoking statement about her busyness interfering with the family's fun.

With that, she flung whatever tool she had in her hand against the wall with such force that it broke. Then she withdrew to her room.

That left me with two horrible feelings: anger and guilt. The pain of that combination induced me to crucify my masculine ego and, as Paul would say, "put on the new man"—put on Jesus Christ. Then, I went to Betsy to tell her of my feelings and my awareness of hers, and that I couldn't stand the separation.

There were a few awful moments—really chilling, frightening moments for me—when she did not respond. The wall remained. But because Betsy, through Christ, is full of grace and truth, she let down the wall. We expressed our love for each other, and in many ways felt closer than we did before the entire stupid episode took place.

True, we both had acted inappropriately. I started it, but both of us had responded improperly, and both of us could have gotten very judgmental about the reactions of the other. But by walking in the light as Christ is in the light, we found restored fellowship with one another.

If All Else Fails

Someone says, "Wonderful, but what if it doesn't work? Are you saying we can always achieve a happy reconciliation?"

Of course not. Whenever two people are involved, one may decide not to do the will of God. Then, no matter what we do, the other person's reactions to us may be destructive. And here is possibly one of the greatest and most difficult temptations a Christian has to face.

Suppose you have actually, by the grace of God and with volitional love, done all of these things I have suggested to build better relationships and to be reconciled with another, and you are rejected, laughed at, ridiculed, and the wall remains.

This situation can produce great bitterness and resentment in the Christian who, up to that point, had been walking in the Spirit. "Why, I've done everything that could possibly be expected of me, and more, and he (she) treats me like this!"

The Bible forewarns we may encounter resistance from those with whom we seek to be reconciled. "It is harder to win back the friendship of an offended brother than to capture a fortified city. His anger shuts you out like iron bars" (Prov. 18: 19).

Jesus pointed out that there is a point at which we should withdraw from our attempts to seek reconciliation (Matt. 18:17). Sometimes a person will not be reconciled. If we continue to push, we only make the situation worse. We must, by the grace of God, recognize that that person is human, and right now he or she can't hear us.

We must not now shift the other way, after acting in love, and become condemning, judgmental, and bitter. Instead, we must continue to pray, and we must remain available. We should be sensitive to any opening that God may give us for reconciliation later. We may be very hesitant, since we have been hurt once, and we may not want to take that chance again. But if we are praying honestly and that person opens the door, we have to be willing to go through and risk it again.

Hard? Yes, but blessed too. As Jesus said, "Blessed are the peacemakers [happy are those who strive for peace], for they shall be called the children of God" (Matt. 5:9, KJV).

Ultimately, however, nothing can guarantee that our words will be needed. It's the power of the Holy Spirit that convicts a person and that reveals the truth to him. In some ways, this should be reassuring to us. It takes much of the pressure off us. While we are responsible for being truthful and for being loving and accepting, it's really not up to us to change anybody. This is the work of the Holy Spirit. So there is no point in getting our egos in an uproar or getting tense and trying to force the relationship in some way. If we are honestly available and are praying for healing of the relationship, we can confidently turn it over to the Holy Spirit and relax.

Dealing with Children

The principles already mentioned are valid in dealing with our anger toward our children, but I want to mention some special aspects of this relationship. I see many parents, particularly mothers, who express great guilt and frustration over how angry they get with their children: "I start the day off yelling, and I end the day yelling. I cry, I pray, I vow not to yell again; but I don't go 30 minutes without another round of screaming."

Ephesians 6:4 says "Do not irritate and provoke your children to anger—do not exasperate them to resentment—but rear them (tenderly) in the training and discipline and the counsel and admonition of the Lord" (AMP). This is not a plea for permissiveness; it's a statement that we should bring our children up lovingly but with discipline.

Many of the headaches and ultimately heartaches we have with our children come because we virtually train them *not* to obey us. We say many things that we don't back up until finally we're in a rage; then they begin to listen.

Suppose you are entertaining company in the living room. The children are watching TV in the family room. TV noises are filtering through to the living room, as are sounds of giggling, scuffling, and wrestling. You excuse yourself from the guests, go in, and tell the children to quiet down.

You return to your guests, and the TV is as loud as ever, as are the children's noises. You go back and say with a little more irritation in your voice, "I thought I told you to be quiet!"

You try to resume your visit with company. About this time apparently some violent murder is occurring on TV, and one of the children hits the floor yelling because his head has been bumped.

Now you go in and yell, "What's the matter with you kids? You act like a bunch of wild people! Didn't you hear me? Here I've got company, and you sound like a madhouse. Now *be quiet!*"

You go back to the living room, and it's quiet. For three to five minutes. Then sounds of violence shatter the brief and blessed peace. At this point, you don't know whether it's the children or the TV, but it doesn't matter. In a towering rage, you stomp into the family room and do your thing, jumping up and down, frothing at the mouth, and dislocating your son's shoulder. Now you at last have their attention, and they're listening to you.

Many of us through the years consistently train our children that they don't have to listen to us until we finally explode. No wonder they develop the habit of paying very little attention to our nagging until that explosive point is reached.

The proper model of loving discipline, suggested

in Ephesians 6:4, would have you go in and have exactly the same conversation you had the first time. But the second time you would go in, turn the TV off, and say, "OK, you haven't been able to be quiet, and we do need it to be quiet now. You'll have to separate, and you won't be able to watch TV the rest of the evening."

The secure parent is not overly intimidated by the cries of angry protest that might follow such action. If we are consistent in teaching our children that there are consequences for misbehavior and that we mean what we say, we will save ourselves much grief later. This approach is less likely to breed resentment than the nagging, scolding style. Ephesians 6:4 is really another Scripture that is directing us to confrontation without condemnation.

In summary then, we must learn to honestly face our anger. We must restrain its uncontrolled and inappropriate expressions, but allow it to motivate us to the kind of action that resolves conflicts or, at least, improves relationships.

We shall then not only have tamed the wild beast but also have harnessed it to our service— and the Lord's.

14

Seven Steps to Untwisted Living

At any given point in time, you or someone very close to you is probably in desperate need of healing—emotionally. In any average assembly of people from church congregation to coffee klatch, from ceramic class to calorie counters club—there are people who are really hurting. Some are depressed; some are despairing. Some, when they pray, feel that no one is there. Some have tremendous anxieties. One or two may have trouble even sitting in the room with the group because of their anxiety, wondering whether they might lose control. Some are in tremendous need of healing because of very destructive emotions: jealousy, resentment, bitterness, lust, greed, despair.

I have learned by talking to ministers of virtually every denomination and by treating people from all walks of life that no one is exempt from this. Whatever one's beliefs may be or whatever commitment one has to the Lord Jesus Christ, no one is exempt from neurotic kinks, internal battles, and sometimes very painful emotions. So there is a great need for untwisting our lives.

1. Believe That God Loves You

When we're in need of untwisting, what is the most basic prerequisite? To some it may seem very evident. Others may not be able to accept it at all. But the simple truth that underlies all healing is that God loves you. This is something that needs to be communicated, experienced, felt, believed.

Mike, a boy in his teen-age years who had been brought up in a Christian home and had always given assent to basic Christian teachings, began to develop more and more a sense that he was worthless, that he could never live up to the expectations of those around him, and that he probably would not "make it" in life. In this frame of mind, Mike began to select companions who in a sense were fellow aliens. Together they got involved in experimentation with drugs, breaking various rules at school, and stealing. This reinforced his negative self-image.

Mike began to agonize over his life style more and more, knowing that he was going down a dead-end street and yet feeling helpless to correct matters. Finally one night he called out to God, asking Him to come into his life, to change him, because he really didn't want to go this route. Suddenly he began to breathe heavily, to look up in disbelief, as God met him. He sensed that he was in the presense of God, that God loved him, that he was acceptable to God, and it was great. His comment: "Wow!"

The next day Mike began to disentangle himself from his more destructive companions. He also began to share with them that God loved them, and that there is more in this life for them than they had yet found. Mike has continued on this path, and has become a living example of the healing power of God's love. He is somebody, and he is worthwhile because God loves him.

God loves you, too, and the proof that He loves you is in Jesus Christ. As Christian scholars such as Pascal and C. S. Lewis suggest, the proof of God's love is not to be found in nature. A person may talk about seeing the love of God in beautiful sunsets, the fall colors, and the fragrant flowers of spring, but that same person must also face the fact of wolves tearing deer to pieces, of people killing each other, of tornadoes and floods and famines. Nature may reveal the majesty, the awesomeness, the unsearchable greatness of God, but you cannot prove by nature that God loves you. And you cannot prove God loves you by any esoteric mysticism.

The ultimate proof that God loves you is in the person of Jesus Christ. Here is God's ultimate identification with us. He became just like we are. To be tempted just as we are. To suffer as we do, and to reveal to us His very nature. And then, the supreme proof of His love is the cross, where He agonized and died to save us from our sins.

All this makes it possible, by our submitting to Christ, to get self off the throne and to be released from the chains of egocentricity. Yes, Jesus Christ is the proof that God loves us, and this is the basic truth of healing. Believe it. Ask the Lord to make His love real to you. Eventually you should be able literally to revel in the fact of God's love and fully experience its magnificent healing power.

2. Admit Your Problems

If the first key word to untwisting life is love, the second is light. The Apostle John wrote, "If we walk in the light as He (Jesus Christ) is in the light, we have fellowship one with another, and the blood of Jesus Christ His Son cleanseth us from all sin" (1 John 1:7, KJV). What does John mean by walking in the light? How does he use the metaphor? And how is "walking in the light" related to having fellowship and being cleansed from all sin?

To understand this, one must consider John's earlier work, his Gospel, in which he presents Jesus Christ as the eternal life-giving force behind everything that exists. And this life "was the *light* of men" (John 1:4, KJV). So to walk in the light is, first of all, to possess the life that comes from Jesus Christ. (Though the life of every man originates in Jesus Christ and is sustained by Him, those who receive Christ have a distinctive spiritual life —and light—through Him.)

The Apostle Paul made use of the same metaphor, writing about "the light of the glorious Gospel of Christ" (2 Cor. 4:4, KJV). Paul said that, in the case of the Christian, "God, who commanded the light to shine out of darkness, hath shined in our hearts, to give the light of the knowledge of the glory of God . . . (v. 6). So, then, we need to *be* in Christ the Light before we can possibly *walk* in the light.

The second principle concerning light is found in the third chapter of John's Gospel, where we are taught that men "loved darkness rather than light" because the light revealed their evil deeds (vv. 19-21). Here, light is used to describe the penetrating, diagnostic, soul-heart revealing insight of Jesus Christ—the living Word of God. To walk in the light, then, would be to subject ourselves to the scrutiny of God's Word, and to honestly admit our sins and faults as they are revealed to us by the Word.

People will often go through fantastic mental gymnastics to hide from the truth—to conceal the truth about themselves, to walk in the dark rather than in the light. Many Christians suffer needlessly because they try to deny that they have any problems. They seem to think that if anybody has an emotional problem he must not be a Christian, or at least not a very good Christian.

Since people who buy this neurotic philosophy cannot admit that they have problems, they wear masks; they play games—and hurt internally. Some are so adept at repressing and denying their problems that they are honestly unaware of them. Yet they may be a museum piece of subtle psychological problems, because negative, hurtful emotions will come out one way or another.

The Apostle John tells us that if we walk in the light we are going to have fellowship with one another; we are going to experience cleansing. The reverse implication is also valid. If we fail to walk in the light, our fellowship will suffer, and we will not experience cleansing. Light has healing effects. As long as we hide our problems in darkness, there is not much hope of healing.

Admittedly, it's painful to expose ourselves to the light, to see what's in us. We would rather hide behind a smiling face, or our decency, or a discreet silence. We can hide from ourselves even in our prayer life. Even with the Lord, we play all kinds of games to avoid exposing ourselves to the light.

For example, we may pray in very broad generalities about the rest of the world. We may use such stereotyped, pious phrases in talking to the

Lord that there is a ring of unreality to our prayers, and our real self is not coming through.

We may make specific petitions for other people, and not deal with our own petty egos.

We have a built-in resistance against recognizing in ourselves that arrogance, that pride, that conceit, that self-centeredness, often so apparent to others who observe us. We feign innocent unawareness of the little ways in which we put down others, or even give the knife to those we love.

We must face these things. We must come into the light of Jesus Christ. It may be convenient or comforting to compare ourselves favorably with someone else, but it's the light of Jesus Christ that really reveals us as we are, and this revelation must absolutely take place for healing.

Jesus Himself also used *light* as a metaphor for direction. If we follow Jesus Christ, He lights our path and we will not stumble (John 8:12). So much anguish that people experience is a direct result of not following the light of Jesus Christ. Sometimes a person gets further and further away from healing when he or she speculates about his or her guilt and its alleged causes. What a person really needs to do is to face the fact that he is behaving in a way that is destructive, to confess it, and to stop it. He needs to turn himself over to Jesus Christ, following the light of His revelation, obeying Him, and then he won't stumble.

Followers of Christ are also described in Scripture as light bearers or light sharers. The Christian who does not share the light of Jesus Christ in word or deed with others, through whatever gifts he has, is not going to experience fullness and the completeness of the power of Jesus Christ. This seems to be both a biological and a spiritual principle. What we don't use we lose. If we don't share, we shrivel. There is no plateau on which we can rest. As is true of all biological systems; the Christian is either progressing or regressing. One of the progressive influences in Christian experience is to share the light we have. There is no such thing as a victorious, *theoretical* Christian. One who intellectually gives assent to spiritual truths but does not live and share the light of Jesus Christ will get nowhere.

What does it mean, then, to walk in the light? If we have the eternal life-giving presence of Jesus Christ within us, if we have turned our lives over to Him, confessing our sins, if we are honestly opening ourselves to Him as a continuing process, if we are obeying the directives of His Word— then we are walking in the light.

Is it not ironic that when a person has a salvation experience he very honestly opens himself up to Jesus Christ, confessing his sin and revealing himself in his great need, but as he goes further in his Christian experience, he often begins, to "fake it instead of make it?" He does not maintain this honesty and openness, and he is not walking in the light anymore. We need to resist this tendency. We need constantly to come out into the light, for this is where healing and forgiveness are for us.

3. Take Personal Responsibility

Another step toward untwisting life is to understand and acknowledge that "out of the heart of man" comes his problems (Matt. 15:19, 20). The trouble is within you, Jesus said. Men will customarily do almost anything to avoid facing this fact. They will blame society, their parents, even

God. ("It's His fault I am the way I am; He made me this way, didn't He?") Some look to astrology and try to blame their aberrations on the stars. But, as Shakespeare wrote, "The fault, dear Brutus, is not in our stars, but in ourselves that we are underlings" (Cassius in *Julius Caesar*).

Yes, Jesus said that the attitudes and behavior patterns from which man requires healing are "out of the heart." Man is defiled from the inside out. So long as we try to see our problems as originating outside ourselves, there is little hope for healing. This idea that if only someone else would do something, or if only my mother or father had done differently, or if I'd only had a better environment, I'd be all right is extremely detrimental. The only hope for the individual lies in realizing that internal change is what is needed. Healing must occur within, where the problems originate.

Unfortunately psychiatry and psychology have contributed to the notion that people are not really responsible for what they do. "You are stimulus-response. You are fighting inevitable conflicts. Your mama didn't love you. You've got problems from the past." When a person is in a very disturbed state or has done something very destructive, the immediate emotional reflex of some counselors is to discover "what caused" the behavior.

I believe a tremendous error has been made in confusing *motivation* with *causation*. It is usually incorrect to say that anybody causes you to do anything. And if you say that, you are already off on a wrong presupposition. And you won't solve the problem.

We really can't say, for example, that someone made us angry. They did not inject anger into our veins. The anger was latent within us all the time

It came from within our being. Someone might have motivated us to be angry, and we reacted to the situation and became angry. But no one made us angry.

We have innumerable motivations that impinge upon us, and we selectively attend to certain ones. Then we may make the very significant error of saying that someone or something made us do thus and so.

As long as we blame circumstances or others, we lose the opportunity to become part of the healing process.

One very interesting phenomenon about which many psychiatrists have written concerns the husband who is an alcoholic. The wife is very upset over this and believes this is the root of all their problems. If only he would quit drinking, then she could love him better, and everything would turn out all right.

Sometimes such a husband does quit drinking. He may have a dramatic Christian experience. Everybody is very proud of him, of what Christ has enabled him to do. Is the wife jumping with joy? Is she praising the Lord? No, she is getting depressed. Her golden bridge, her perfect excuse, has been taken away. For years she had lived under the delusion that if only he would quit drinking, all their problems would be solved. He's quit drinking, and she's the same old self. With her same bitterness, resentment, jealousies, and problems. Only now she doesn't have a golden bridge to explain her problems, so she is depressed.

A song by Anna Russell expresses more eloquently than I can this syndrome of people not taking personal responsibility for their behavior problems:

"I went to my psychiatrist
   to be psychoanalyzed,
To find out why I killed the cat
   and blackened my wife's eyes.

He put me on a downy couch
   To see what he could find,
And this is what he dredged up
   From my subconscious mind:

When I was one, my mommy hid
   My dolly in the trunk,
And so it follows naturally,
   That I am always drunk.

When I was two, I saw my father
   Kiss the maid one day,
And that is why I suffer now—
   kleptomania.

When I was three, I suffered from
   Ambivalence toward my brothers,
So it follows naturally,
   I poisoned all my lovers.

I'm so glad that I have learned
   The lesson it has taught,
That everything I do that's wrong
   Is someone else's fault!"

There is really little hope of healing if we don't take the responsibility for ourselves and say, "OK, I'm hurting. What can I do to help change things?" If you wait around for someone else to change, you will prolong suffering. Your greatest hope is that you change. As many authorities, both Christian and non-Christian have perceived the basic issue is not the circumstance of people but their reaction to it.

What are your reactions? What role do you play, ironically, in producing the very things that you don't like? People often help cause what they seem to hate most, the things that cause the greatest trouble for them. This is one of the insights I try to help a person gain. This is not putting the person down. This is not being judgmental or cruel or unsympathetic. If this approach is taken properly, it is communicating that there *is* hope. Regardless of whether others change or not, there is hope from within yourself. Your changed role could significantly change the situation.

A person must take personal responsibility and ask himself some serious questions. *How can I react differently? How can I creatively bring the Lord Jesus Christ into my life, into my reactions, into this situation?* This leads to healing. This is a crucial step, and if this step is not taken, you'll most likely not find healing.

4. Believe That You Can Change

A fourth basic step to untwisting your life is to *believe that change is possible for you.*

Betty was a young woman who had had an unsatisfactory relationship with her father. She did not trust him; she did not trust her husband; nor did she trust God. She had a fatalistic attitude that she had one type personality, her husband had another, and they were simply incompatible.

The implication was that nothing could be done. Furthermore, she seemed to feel that she had an irreversible psychological trauma as a result of having had a bad relationship with her father, and so she couldn't expect to have a good relationship with God or her husband.

Betty cannot find healing until she realizes she has a choice in what she does. She can either make a commitment to her husband and to God, or not. She does not have to be controlled by feelings. If instead of feeling that she is a pawn in the hands of fate, she begins to meet her commitments, her feelings will change.

Until then, she is travelling down a dead-end street. For the Christian, the fatalistic, nothing-can-be-done attitude constitutes a practical denial of faith. Having Jesus Christ within gives a new principle, an entirely new attitude, new motivations, new capacities for love, new obedience, new values to uphold.

The personality change that Christ can bring to an individual through personal conversion is a very well-known phenomenon. The Apostle Paul said, "Therefore if any man be in Christ, he is a new creature; old things are passed away, behold all things are become new" (2 Cor. 5:17, KJV). Many people who are virtual stereotypes of what some consider sinners—drunkards, gamblers, thieves, or immoral people—have experienced, upon receiving Christ, the dramatic change this verse describes. There is no question that change is possible, even when deeply engrained habits and attitudes of a lifetime are involved.

Unfortunately, many Christians, both those who have experienced dramatic, life-changing conversions and those whose regeneration has come about more quietly, have not applied the life-changing principles of Christianity to many areas of life.

A man may have quit drinking the day he was saved but still have a preoccupation with his work or pleasure, to the neglect of his family. A woman may have forever renounced promiscuity when she came to know Christ but still may compulsively spend her husband's money or be a slave to self-pity or vanity.

Very often, we forfeit any possibility for change in regard to the subtle sins, the sins of the spirit, bad attitudes and negative thinking, because we somehow don't really believe that change in these areas is possible for us. We say that this is just the way we are.

We claim to know and understand what sin is, and profess to have turned from our sins. The actual fact may be, however, that we have turned from the stereotype sins condemned by society (church or civil) but not from the sins of the spirit.

Here is a person obsessed with worry. Is there any hope for change? Certainly, but change is not likely to come unless and until the worrier *believes* he can change. And belief, in turn, may not come until one has faced the fact that his worry is directly contrary to the Word of God, which says, "Be careful [or anxious] for nothing, but in every thing by prayer and supplication, with thanksgiving, let your requests be made known unto God, and the peace of God which passeth all understanding shall keep your hearts and minds through Christ Jesus" (Phil. 4:6, 7, KJV).

The same thing is true of neurotic fear, self-pity, inferiority feelings, conceit, envy, discontent.

Throughout the Scriptures, great emphasis is put on faith. In fact, Scripture goes so far as to say that "without faith it is impossible to please" God (Heb. 11:6, KJV).

It also says that the person who wavers because of unbelief will not receive anything from the Lord (see James 1:5-8). It is no wonder, then, that we must believe change is possible before we can expect to experience much healing in our own personal lives.

Actually, many people have a *negative* faith. They *believe* all right, but they believe the wrong things. They believe that they are the way they are because they were "just born that way." They believe that they would be simply pretending if they even tried to change. They believe that they will be as they are now until the day they die. Far from lacking faith, they have strong faith. And their faith is producing the very negative and destructive things that make them and their loved ones unhappy.

"According to your faith be it unto you," Jesus said (Matt. 9:29, KJV). That is true whether your faith is in your *inability* to change, with perpetual sorrow being the result, or in the possibility of change through Christ, with increasing joy being the result.

These contrasting paths are described in Proverbs. "But the path of the just is as the shining light, that shineth more and more unto the perfect day. The way of the wicked is as darkness; they know not at what they stumble" (Prov. 4:18, 19, KJV). The more and more shining path is for those who believe change is possible for them through Jesus Christ. Will you believe it?

5. Pray Honestly

The fifth step toward untwisted living has to do with prayer. Most people who know what prayer is all about and whose personal experiences seem to back it up share one thing in common: they pray very specifically. None of this, "Help me to be a better mother/father," or, "Help me to be a better Christian."

Instead, they pray, "Lord, help me at the breakfast table this morning to somehow express love to the children and to be more aware of the first signs of rising irritability that usually end with me screaming. Help to deal with it constructively," or "When my husband comes home tonight, give us a chance to share, and help me to be more aware of his needs."

Roger had epilepsy as a child and was frequently embarrassed because he would lose control of himself. He never had a close relationship with his father and was reared primarily by a rather stern and, according to him, unloving grandmother.

Roger outgrew his epileptic condition, but as an adult he had fear of heights, fear of sharp objects, fear of close places, fear of driving. All of these fears basically related to his deeper fear that he might lose control of himself.

He had problems in giving and receiving love, and a great deal of his fear centered around suddenly harming someone. As he recognized the origin of his fears and all that was behind them, he could begin to pray more specifically. He was no longer fighting a phantom.

He could pray specifically for healing of the sense of shame and fear that came from the period when he had epileptic seizures. As specific fears arose, he learned to thank the Lord for the situation and to really identify himself as a child of God and a joint heir with Christ. This enabled him to command out specific fears. While this did not always immediately relieve the fear, he had the assurance that he was at least not giving Satan a foothold, and this in itself gave him confidence.

I believe the Lord honors specific prayers. And I think there is something to praying with one's feelings. I'm very impressed with the Book of Habakkuk and the example it gives of praying with feeling. You won't hear the tone that Habakkuk used at the average church service or prayer meeting. Someone stands up to pray, and from the voice intonations and what is said, you get the impression the person is delivering some kind of sermon or address into a microphone and that possibly there is nothing higher than the electronic device on the other end to hear it. Habakkuk prayed as if somebody was listening, and he expressed his feelings.

Do you know what he said? "Lord, what's the matter? I've been praying and praying and You don't hear me; You don't answer me. I shout, HELP! MURDER! VIOLENCE! and nothing happens. It all seems to be in vain. Where are You?" (see Hab. 1:2).

Does this kind of praying work? Imbedded in Habakkuk is one of the greatest truths ever revealed to mankind. The entire Book of Romans was based upon this truth. Later, the Protestant Reformation occurred because this truth became a creative, motivating, driving voice in the back of Martin Luther's head. "The just shall live by his faith" (Hab. 2:4, KJV; cf. Rom. 1:17).

After Habakkuk disclosed his feelings, revealing himself before the Lord as we have described, he closed his book with one of the greatest expressions of faith you'll find in the Scriptures. "Even though the fig trees are all destroyed and . . . the olive crops all fail . . . even if the flocks die in the fields and the cattle barns are empty, yet will I rejoice in the Lord. I will be happy in the

God of my salvation. The Lord is my Strength, and He will give me the speed of a deer and bring me safely over the mountains" (Hab. 3:17-19).

These words flowed from the heart and pen of a man who had a personal acquaintance with the Lord! From a man who talked to God honestly and openly. And we need to follow his example.

I think David, also, was shouting in some of the psalms, and not shouting for joy either. Like David, we need to come to the Lord in honesty and in truthfulness and really tell Him where we are and how we feel. We must bring things out into the light; we must get specific.

While it is crucial to be honest in our prayers as Habakkuk and David were, we also need to give thanks whatever our situation. As the Scripture says, "No matter what happens, always be thankful, for this is God's will for you who belong to Christ Jesus" (1 Thes. 5:18).

Even though we may feel terrible about the situation, it is legitimate to give thanks as we are aware that God loves us and that Romans 8:28 is in fact true: "All things work together for good to them that love God, to them who are the called according to His purpose" (KJV).

It is, therefore, not hypocritical to praise the Lord and thank Him for all situations. We need *both* honesty and thankfulness in prayer. Some people thank the Lord hypocritically and are not honest about their feelings. Others get all down in the mouth, pleading, begging, and crying over their situation and do not give thanks.

Regarding interpersonal relations, we should pray to see what we can do differently: "Lord, help me see where I do play a role in this problem. I've been thinking it's all his or her fault. Show me how I can do differently. Show me where my reactions are inappropriate. Help me accept that other person without a lot of riders on the insurance policy. How come I add so much fine print? How come I insist that the policy read, 'I'll love you if . . .' and then I list 10 or 15 changes that are crucial for that person to make before they can really have my love and concern? Lord, help me just to love creatively. Help *me* change." Specific prayers like these are what people need to bring healing.

This kind of praying, however, must also involve a commitment for action. You see, prayer can be used neurotically. As a matter of fact there is no principle in the Scripture or anywhere that you'll ever hear or read that does not have its neurotic abuse, a slight twist or kink that makes it no longer truth, that makes it no longer constructive.

It won't do to stop at praying, "Lord, forgive me for getting so angry at my wife, hurting her, cutting her down because I know where she is vulnerable. I let her have it, but forgive me, Lord." To stop there is a cop-out, a neurotic abuse of prayer.

I must go to my wife and ask forgiveness and correct this situation, making restitution by creatively showing love to her. Who am I kidding by asking the Lord to forgive me if I don't put myself into action? When we pray for the Lord to reveal our failings and His truth to us, we need a commitment—a radical commitment to vigorous action. Go to a person you have wronged, and ask him to forgive you.

6. We Must Forgive

The sixth step toward an untwisted life has to

do with forgiveness. As long as we harbor an unforgiving spirit or resentment, we cannot expect much healing. This is a principle that Christ made clear (see Matt. 6:15). If you don't forgive others, you won't be forgiven. As a psychiatrist, I can verify that people who are harboring unforgiving spirits often have difficulty in feeling forgiven, whether in an absolute sense before God they may be or not. Possibly the dynamic of this is that since they do not forgive others, it is inconceivable to them that they can be forgiven.

Ray and Jean Johnson were Christians, but Ray felt he was far away from God, and he could not seem to get close. He had difficulty believing that God loved him or heard his prayers. He felt estranged from God.

Ray had a very bitter, unforgiving spirit toward his wife. He had a collection of grievances against her that went back for 10 years. She had gone out with another man one time; she never paid any attention to him; she was always busy with her friends, club meetings, and other things.

Ray expressed a very definite conviction that there was hope for their marriage only if his wife changed. He felt there was nothing he could do to correct the problems in their marriage, that it was all up to Jean.

Ray didn't see how he could forgive his wife unless she would change. He had trouble understanding that his judging, critical spirit motivated Jean to be busy with other things because they brought some sense of worth. His exclusive focus on changes she should make, coupled with an unforgiving spirit, separated him from God and from his wife.

If healing is to take place, we must forgive. We must confess our resentment and hurt. We must

go to others who have hurt us and seek reconciliation.

We also need the experience of saying, "Yes, I
forgive you," to others who come to us. Have you
ever had someone apologize to you, and you have
said, "Oh, that's all right; it didn't bother me at
all"? Don't let yourself get away with that. That's
pride. That's a problem you've got. It did bother
you. You need to have the grace to say, "Yes, that
really bothered me. I appreciate your asking forgiveness, and I forgive you. I want our relationship
to be better. There has been this little undercurrent
of resentment."

We need this kind of honesty. Other people need
to have the experience of forgiving too. This means
we should actively seek forgiveness as well as forgiving others. How destructive are the injustices
we collect in disobedience to God's law of love.
There are many people who are avid injustice collectors. To be healed, we need to pour out these
feelings and injustices, bring them out into the
light, nail them to the cross of Christ, and be
cleansed.

7. Learn Discipline of Mind
The last step in appropriating God's power for
untwisted living involves developing an entirely
new mind toward yourself, toward people, toward
circumstances. This requires mental discipline. This
is not something that just happens. As a matter
of fact, the passive person will never develop his
potential. Life is an active warfare against destructive influences. The sources of such influences include our own egocentricity, Satan, and, sometimes,
other people.

The admonition to actively resist evil runs

throughout the Scriptures. We are to put on the full armor of God (Eph. 6:10-18). Have you ever noticed that this classic passage describes no protection for the back? We must wage an offensive warfare. The passive Christian who turns his back has no protection. He's going to go down to defeat.

We often don't have a full enough appreciation of the power of the forces of darkness. This is spiritual warfare in which we are engaged. We wrestle not with flesh and blood but with powers and principalities. The devil is like a roaring lion that seeks to devour whom he may. He attempts to accomplish this by attacking us where we are vulnerable. Therefore we must be very aware of our vulnerable areas, for the "Roaring Lion" will always be lurking to take advantage of the situation. To counter our own foibles and Satan's efforts to capitalize on them, we must have an ongoing process of prayer.

Paul told the Thessalonians to pray without ceasing. He also told them if they didn't work, they wouldn't eat. I presume, therefore, that by "unceasing prayer" Paul meant something other than being on our knees in prayer 24 hours a day. I think he was talking about a mind set, an attitude, an awareness, an ongoing mental process by which one is constantly tuned in to God.

This process prayer can work as follows: If our vulnerable area is exposed and under attack, we reidentify who we are—sons of God, joint heirs with Christ—and reaffirm our commitment to Him.

Next, we thank God for His power and love, for who we are in Him, and even for the circumstances ("Always be thankful no matter what happens"— 1 Thes. 5:18). Even though we don't like the circumstances, we can legitimately praise God for them, resting in the knowledge that ultimately all things work together for good for those who love God and are fitting into His plans (see Rom. 8:28).

Next, we command Satan to be bound, for greater is He who is in us than he who is in the world (see 1 John 4:4). Now we can actually cast out whatever emotion is developing in our vulnerable area, and we should do so very specifically: "In the name of the Lord Jesus Christ, I rebuke you and cast you out, you spirit of lust, greed, jealousy, pride, whatever."

If we have given ground to Satan, we now reclaim our relationship in the name of Christ.

Finally, under the Lordship of Jesus Christ, we actively go counter to the pull of Satan and our egocentricity. For example, if someone is putting us down and our vulnerable area is pride, we can bring process prayer into action by quickly re-identifying who we are in Christ, thanking God for the situation, resisting Satan, casting out the spirit of pride, and going counter to the egocentric pull which would normally lead us to putting the other person down in some way. Instead, we give him the gift of listening and let him know we understand his viewpoint.

With this new mind set, we can view people and circumstances as opportunities to live Jesus Christ and to practice love no matter what the circumstance. So many people have the opposite mind set: people and circumstances are a perpetual burden to them. I face people every day who seem to be overwhelmed with life. Everything that comes their way is a burden. Life is such a problem, and even the quality of their prayer is, "Lord, deliver me." All they seem to know is the "Help-me-to-get-through-one-more-day" kind of prayer.

Judy was a young married lady who had been dreadfully afraid of having cancer or going crazy for many years. She also had many other phobias, and she was frequently depressed.

When Judy became a Christian she gained a greater sense of worth and some sense of security, but her fears and depression continued. She got into therapy with me, and obtained significant relief from her depression by means of medications. (There is a type of depression that is chemical.) She also began to deal with her fears, both through psychotherapy techniques and through learning how to become more and more specific in turning her fears over to the Lord in prayer.

Finally she overcame most of her fears. She felt that if she were a strong enough Christian, she should be able to stop the medications. However, when she attempted to stop the medications, she became depressed. She felt defeated, felt that she was not a good Christian, and maybe God was really not there, or, if He were, He didn't reach down to her.

Judy engaged in rather agonizing prayer over a period of time, pleading with God to take her depression away. She had an element of spiritual pride in all this, wanting to be able to testify to the fact that she was so strong in the Lord that she no longer had to take medications.

However, the fact was that she did need medications, and she got back on them. The final point of deliverance came to her when she could pray, "Lord, even if I have to stay depressed the rest of my life and take pills the rest of my life, I will praise You. I will let You be God. I thank You for the situation, and I turn myself over to You." When she got to that point, the depression lifted. I anticipate now being able to stop the medications gradually.

Decide now that you will not be a poor-mouth Christian. Decide that no matter what happens, no matter what comes your way, it is an opportunity to practice love, to learn to pray. This can really change a person's life. It is part of a process of healing, of maturing, of growth.

I'm not talking about some flashing insight by which it is suddenly all there—Zap! I'm talking about a process. We are predestined, Paul says, to be conformed to the image of Jesus Christ. This process will never be fully realized until we are with Him in eternity.

We are saved for eternity when we believe that Jesus Christ is who He said He was and we trust Him as Lord and Saviour. But salvation is also a process of being saved from the chains of ego-centricity.

We are never fully and finally free in this life. But there are relative degrees of freedom in the process of healing. And the person who knows he is loved, who brings what's inside into the light, who takes personal responsibility for his problems, who believes change is possible through Christ, who prays honestly, who forgives and seeks forgiveness, and who practices discipline of mind and process prayer will make great strides toward untwisting his life and moving toward his rightful destiny: to be conformed to the image of Christ.